68070

65

Ⅱ0560980

# PASTORAL CARE
## AND
# PASTORAL THEOLOGY

# PASTORAL
# CARE
# AND
# PASTORAL
# THEOLOGY

## by IAN F. McINTOSH

## w
## THE WESTMINSTER PRESS
Philadelphia

ISBN 0–664–20924–6

Library of Congress Catalog Card No. 71–169599

PUBLISHED BY THE WESTMINSTER PRESS®
PHILADELPHIA, PENNSYLVANIA

PRINTED IN THE UNITED STATES OF AMERICA

To Seward Hiltner

# CONTENTS

# ACKNOWLEDGMENTS

There are too many people whose formative influence on my life has contributed to my arrival at this point for it to be possible to list them. Seward Hiltner, to whom this book is dedicated, will alone be mentioned. For he took an unknown British minister into his doctoral program on trust, and guided him through to completion. Also, the very concept of pastoral theology with which I wrestle in these pages is his more than anyone else's.

Several people have helped directly in the preparation of the book, and deserve mention. Mrs. Claudia Blue typed the final manuscript. Lonnie Dillard, my student assistant, responded to various drafts and read the final proofs. And I am especially grateful to Stuart D. Currie and Prescott H. Williams, Jr. Friends as well as colleagues, they read almost the whole of the penultimate version and offered many penetrating insights and suggestions.

# INTRODUCTION

It is customary for a play or a detective story to be prefaced by a list of the characters in order of their appearance, sometimes with the addition of a brief statement about who they are. Mr. and Mrs. Jackson, the other characters in this book, will become as well known to the reader as they are to me as the conversations with them proceed. But it seems desirable to say a word or two about myself at this point.

What is relevant to the book is that I see my primary vocational commitment in terms of the parish ministry. Inasmuch as I have pursued academic studies considerably beyond the B.D. level and have taught for a time in a Presbyterian seminary, I am presumably atypical. Yet this is by no means merely a sentimental claim, nor an empty gesture to "the men on the front line." Before this book sees the light of day, I shall have completed the process of returning to the parish ministry—and shall have difficulty finding time to read it, much like the rest of you!

Included for me in this sense of identity is the taxing requirement of being both a pastor and a theologian. (Indeed, it is my conviction that this double task is incumbent upon every Christian, at whatever level he is able to pursue it.)

Throughout the book the diffidence of a generalist at venturing
into such deep waters will make itself felt, even though I
have tried to tone it down at the urging of my friends. My
own theological position falls within the Reformed tradition,
and probably owes most to Scottish theologians such as John
and Donald Baillie and George Hendry, and to H. H. Farmer,
an English Presbyterian who was my teacher.

This book is offered to fellow ministers. In addition to my
own enthusiasm and desire for "feedback," there are three
primary reasons that have motivated me to seek publication,
three aspects of it that I trust merit particular attention.

Most basic of all is the importance that I attach to the task
of "pastoral theology" in the sense in which Seward Hiltner
has given that term a justification and a method.[1] More than
a decade has passed since his seminal contribution was published, yet despite all the tributes that have been paid to it,
the dearth of published materials embodying such pastoral
theology is plain. Lapsley has recently remarked on it, and
MacDonald has suggested that it is a consequence of attention
having been focused on the data of related fields rather than
on the study of actual pastoral operations.[2] In the present
volume, not only is the theological reflection tied to a concrete
pastoral situation but it genuinely starts from there—and to
the best of my knowledge this marks it off from almost all that
has been published in the field. Even Thornton, whose fine
book comes perhaps as close as anything else to what Hiltner
was pleading for, has a central issue in mind to which he is
addressing himself and uses his pastoral material as docu-
mentary evidence.[3] Here, in contrast, the given pastoral situation is the focus, and all the analysis and discussion will flow
from it in whatever direction it dictates. The pastoral ministry
is not being used to illustrate a theme, but to discover the
theme.

The second aspect of this book, an immediately practical
one, is the original reason that prompted me to pursue the

matter beyond the initial theological analysis for my personal use. While this point is closely related to the concept of "pastoral theology," it does not depend upon the methodological justification of such an endeavor. It is the apparently simple fact that thinking about the first pastoral conversation theologically led me to see the situation somewhat differently in terms of the future ministry indicated. This was so despite the fact that my background of reading and experience in psychology and clinical pastoral education is more extensive than that of the average minister. This is not to deny that anyone more versed in psychology, or with greater skill in the art of pastoral conversation, or simply blessed with more insight, might have managed perfectly well without such an effort. Nor is it intended to beg the question of the accuracy of the actual theological analysis. It is simply to take seriously the fact that for most ministers, theology is the language and perspective in which they are "at home," and which is accordingly likely to be the most effective tool at their disposal in the analysis of pastoral conversations. The validity of this position is not explicitly argued, but it is hoped that the present book demonstrates something of its value and possibilities. With respect to both this and the previous part of the rationale, it is the *method* on which I am staking my coat. If the content is illuminating too, that is a bonus.

The third reason for offering the extensive verbatim of a pastoral ministry may seem rather a strange one—namely, that it is not by any stretch of the imagination a "success story." At the time these conversations took place, the author had had a year of clinical pastoral education, supervised the pastoral ministry of a number of future ministers, and had a few years of parish experience. Yet the consensus of those reading this book (it has been that of numerous students responding to parts of the book, unaware of the writer's identity) may well be that the minister is a zealot, needing a good, swift kick plus a first quarter of clinical pastoral education.

But the motive for presenting it still holds. Undoubtedly some who are ordained ministers are naturally gifted with great compassion and understanding, and others benefit from skilled supervision to improve their natural gifts to a considerably greater degree. Still, it seems reasonable to suspect that pastoral opportunities are frequently mangled, and all too rarely made the most of.

Yet this might never be inferred from the literature, except where concocted responses or brief excerpts from the verbatims of beginners are cited as horrible examples of what not to do. And granted that success has something to teach us, so does failure. Fosdick has somewhere observed that a man who is bitten twice by the same dog is more fitted to that occupation than any other. Thornton has offered a model of courageous acknowledgment of pastoral failure, albeit in summary form.[4] I do not particularly enjoy exposing my mistakes to others (that's known as "British understatement," by the way!). But perhaps there is truth in some words of Leland Elhard: "Often we are ashamed of our broken pastoral language, and we hide it because it does not measure up in elegance to other branches of theological study. From the existentialists we learn that our battle-scarred language is what it is because it still carries in it the sounds and smells of action. We should properly treasure it as conveying the messages of God and man."[5] So this account of a ministry is offered, as Oliver Cromwell reputedly insisted that his portrait should be painted, "warts and all."

The arrangement of the book is as follows. Chapters I–III each contain a segment (distinguished by time or person) of the pastoral relationship with members of the Jackson family, together with analyses from both a pastoral care and a theological standpoint. Chapter IV then addresses itself to a number of issues for pastoral care arising explicitly out of the situation but capable of being treated more generally and seeming to be of importance to the pastor. Chapter V follows the same procedure with respect to issues of pastoral theology, and also takes up some of the methodological considerations inherent in such a venture.

Certain limitations, both of the basic document and of the commentary, have to be acknowledged. Whatever the weight or validity of the single case (cf. Chapters IV and V), these verbatims do not cover all the visits with the Jacksons. Quite crucial interchange may thus have passed unrecognized and unrecorded. Even those conversations which do appear, although they were written down very soon after the event, reflect the fallibility and unconscious distortions of memory. A not unrealistic feature, though it will frustrate those who like to peek at the end of a book to discover how the situation turns out, is that the lives of the Jacksons are left in midair, as it were, where the pastoral relationship came to an end.

One further limitation is that only rudimentary and relatively unsystematic reflection upon these conversations took place at the time. That is to say that the extensive deliberate analysis presented here was not available in time to influence successive visits or to be tested in the course of them. Even now, of course, the commentary is by no means exhaustive of all the possibilities of interpretation. For example, the pastoral care observations are almost entirely from a basically Rogerian standpoint. In the last resort, the commentary is reflection on the points and issues that have struck the author as important, illuminating, puzzling, or insoluble, and there is ample scope for others to pursue significant areas on which there has been no elaboration.

As it happens, Mr. and Mrs. Jackson are both now dead. Nevertheless, all distinguishing features have been disguised in the text in order to respect the privacy of their family and friends.

# I

# MRS. JACKSON—JANUARY

### INTRODUCTION

Mrs. Jackson is an active, competent, forty-five-year-old occupational therapist, whom I have known since I became the Free Church chaplain (part time) at Wilton General Hospital, a year ago. As I took up this work, she was not only personally cordial but also helpful in introducing me to some of the hospital staff and employees. My occasional professional contacts with her were supplemented at times when members of her family were hospitalized. However, while I sought to show my concern and she made no secret of her distress, we never sat down privately to talk about it. There was evident mutual respect. But I saw her as a rather capable woman who was managing to stagger along under her load, and was not reaching out for my help. I was also quite conscious of the fact that she was a faithful member of St. Peter's, with a priest of her own.

Mrs. Jackson had been showing physical signs of increasing strain over the past few months. A week off now and then had been insufficient to help, for the situation causing the strain was unchanged upon her return. Indeed, just being left to

look after the rest of the family while Mrs. Jackson took a
week's vacation precipitated the oldest daughter's hospitalization for acute anxiety a month previous to this. I had kept
in touch with the priest at St. Peter's, informing him when
members of the Jackson family were admitted to the hospital,
and I knew that he visited them regularly. On the last such
occasion, I expressed my grave concern for Mrs. Jackson herself, to alert him to this, and he expressed his intention of
making himself more available to her. When I telephoned
him to notify him that she was in the hospital, he told me
that when he had seen her the day before she had looked
like a "walking corpse" and had told him of the possibility
that she would be admitted.

I visited Mrs. Jackson on the day she came into the hospital,
and she said she was pleased I had come. She was rather
drowsy as a result of sedation, but in the course of a seven- or
eight-minute visit did explain that she had been seeing a psychiatrist for some time. "Originally I was going to see him
about my children, but recently he became concerned about
me, and decided that he wanted me to come in for a rest."
She also mentioned that when she had been doing her training, someone had told her that she was a perfectionist. Since
she had not taken Holy Communion for several weeks, and
it had been meaningful to her when she was in the hospital
for an operation several years previously, she asked me if I
would mind calling her priest to let him know that she would
like to receive the Sacrament. She also asked if I would visit
her again the following day, if I could spare the time. The
following verbatim is an account of a thirty-minute visit with
Mrs. Jackson on the following day.

### CONVERSATION

*Minister:*     1   Do you feel up to a visit this afternoon, Mrs.
                    Jackson?

*Mrs. J.:*  2  I'd like it, if you can spare the time. I had been hoping you would come. By the way, thank you for going to the trouble of calling Father Dawson. He came last night and administered the Sacrament, and it was very helpful.

*Minister:*  3  It was no trouble to telephone him, and I'm glad you found it meaningful to receive Communion.

*Mrs. J.:*  4  I don't know him too well yet. I knew his predecessor for many years. He was a fine scholar and a wonderful man.

*Minister:*  5  You must have missed him when he went. Father Dawson came about six months ago, didn't he?

*Mrs. J.:*  6  He did. And he seems an excellent man. (*There followed a lengthy discourse on the advantages and disadvantages of the way in which congregations get ministers in her denomination.*) Did I ever tell you that the older children and I went to a church and Sunday school of your denomination for several years?

*Minister:*  7  I don't believe you did. Was this due to where you were living at the time?

*Mrs. J.:*  8  Yes. There was not one of our churches nearby. My husband was not much of a churchgoer in those days, so I used to take them myself. We got to know the young minister—he had been to Westoak Theological College—and found him very good. I think Father Dawson will be a good pastor too. He listens to what you have to say.

*Minister:*  9  Yes, my impression from contacts with him has been that he doesn't talk unless he has something to say.

*Mrs. J.:*    10    He is a little shy, it seems. But a good pastor can be so much help. I've tried to play God too long. There was the job. And everyone in the family looks to me. And now I've had to give in. I couldn't take it any longer. It's hell living in a soap opera. I couldn't manage anymore.

*Minister:*    11    You had had just about all you could take of being the strong one whom everyone turned to.

*Mrs. J.:*    12    Yes, I had. I don't know how professional people, like ministers, stand it. How do you manage?

*Minister:*    13    Well, in theory there is a clear dividing line between being concerned, and getting so involved that you are torn up by it. It's like with the funeral of someone in your congregation whom you have come to know and love. You may feel you want to express your grief too—but if you do so too much, you will be no help to the mourners in the family. In practice, it's sometimes hard to know where to draw the line. But the second thing is: perhaps we can give ourselves to a person in need with undivided attention and complete concern for an hour. But then we go off to a church meeting or something else. We don't have to live with it and in it all the time.

*Mrs. J.:*    14    Uh-huh, I see. And it's like that for psychiatrists too, I suppose. It certainly is hell living *in* a soap opera. But things will be better now. This rest is certainly doing me good. You've been a great help, and I hope I'll be able to manage.

Minister:    15    (*Feeling that this was rather like an unre-
                   formed alcoholic's promise never to touch an-
                   other drop, and intentionally raising the ques-
                   tion of why she thinks it will be different this
                   time*) But the circumstances haven't changed
                   much, have they?

Mrs. J.:     16    Well, at home they are improving. My hus-
                   band has a job now. The pay is not marvel-
                   ous, but it's reasonable. Of course at the mo-
                   ment he has only been in it a week, and he
                   is still feeling his way. But it will use his
                   creative talents as an advertiser, and it should
                   be quite a challenge. And the oldest teen-
                   ager is all right now. In fact she has quite a
                   sense of humor. I didn't know that until re-
                   cently. I think that is what has helped me at
                   times, to be able to laugh about things.

Minister:    17    Yes. I don't know whether this could be called
                   a means of grace, theologically, but it cer-
                   tainly is in practice! It helps you drain off
                   some of the feelings that otherwise would
                   come out in some other way.

Mrs. J.:     18    Yes. And because I was losing my sense of
                   humor at home, I knew I was wearing pretty
                   thin. When everything piled up, I would
                   sometimes get violently angry. Of course, at
                   times it was so bad that we would all just
                   collapse in laughter. Now the eighteen-year-
                   old . . .

Minister:    19    (*Confused and seeking to clarify*) Oh, you
                   *were* talking about the twenty-one-year-old.

Mrs. J.:     20    Yes. Excuse me, I'm all behind.

Minister:    21    I enjoyed my visit with her a few weeks ago,
                   and was quite impressed with her maturity.

Mrs. J.:     22    She's a good girl. She's looking for a job just

now, but she'll be fine. But Lily, the next one,
is being torn apart. You didn't meet her, did
you? She was only here a few days after taking the overdose, and then was in the mental
hospital for a month. (*Quite open and seemingly acceptant about this.*) She is all over
everything, and we can't suit her at home. (*I
didn't understand this completely.*) She is
caught between the two children of our near
neighbors. The mother is an alcoholic, and
absolutely voracious. Their older one is the
same age as Lily, and on the advice of the
psychiatrist we have asked the school not to
put them in the same class. The younger is
practically totally dependent on Lily. . . .
(*More description of the neighbors.*) Lily has
been confirmed. And I'm sure she has a basic
faith underneath. But she's at the age where
she is rebelling. But I always think that if
they have an underlying faith it will come
back.

*Minister:*   23   You think she is going through an adolescent
stage of questioning the way the church puts
things, but is working through to personal beliefs.

*Mrs. J.:*   24   Yes, and I believe that her faith will win
through. But the younger ones are complete
heathens now. I used to get the older girls
to Sunday school regularly, but I just haven't
had the energy with them. On top of everything else I just haven't been able to see to
it. They are just little heathens, I suppose,
though I do say their prayers with them every
night.

*Minister:*   25   You really have been overloaded with everything, and all the responsibility.

*Mrs. J.:*  26  Yes, I have. I thought of talking to you about it before. But I felt I shouldn't. One of the things about working here is that you see so many people worse off than yourself, and carrying awful burdens—you feel that you ought to be able to carry on. But I shouldn't have tried to play God so long. Then perhaps I would not be here.

*Minister:*  27  Well, there are two things about making these comparisons. In the first place, people differ in their innate capacity to tolerate burdens and strains. But even more important, there is a sense in which long illness and suffering or death are easier to take. They are specific, and often limited—so that they may not be as frustrating as these confused total situations where one cannot see any way out.

*Mrs. J.:*  28  Yes, that's true. There have been times when I have wished that I could just really be ill, and gladly put up with it. But I've always been so healthy that no one realizes. And now I've had to give in. But a good pastor is a great help. You are a good pastor. I think so.

*Minister:*  29  Thank you. This, to me, is the heart of my work as a minister. Not that preaching and teaching are not important. They are. But people with heavy loads, however great their faith, may find it hard to feel that God is with them and helping them when things get overpowering. It seems to me that by my concern and effort genuinely to understand, I can help make God's love and care concrete —and so make it more real to them.

*Mrs. J.:*  30  Well, I certainly feel better since I gave up trying to do it all, and came in here for a rest. I've got a very leaning family.

*Minister:*   31   Yes. And *you* need to be able to share the burden at times—if not with your family, then with your pastor or chaplain or someone.

*Mrs. J.:*    32   I certainly appreciate all the time you have taken. It has done me a lot of good to be able to share this.

*Minister:*   33   That is why I am here as the church's appointed chaplain, generally speaking. And more than that, I have been concerned for you personally. (*At this point I seriously considered suggesting that we pray together, but although it would have been appropriate, there was a deep reflective silence and it did not seem particularly called for.*) I will not be back until Wednesday, and I don't know whether you will still be here then. If you are, I'll certainly be up to see you.

*Mrs. J.:*    34   I don't know, but I hope so. I feel I need a few more days' rest before I can go back to face it all.

*Minister:*   35   I hope so, too, so that you will be *fully* well. I shall be remembering you in my prayers. God bless you.

## PASTORAL CARE

Despite my having had a "pastoral" concern for this woman, in retrospect I would say I felt that her priest had some sort of "prior claim." Neither he nor she ever indicated that there was any problem here, but I was working on the implicit assumption that I should not attempt to activate a pastoral ministry to this woman without exceptionally clear indications that she wished it. Until the day of this conversation, I had never picked up signs of any such explicit reaching out on her part. And Mrs. Jackson's comment (26) would seem to confirm that there had not been any. She had considered it as a possibility, but decided against it for reasons of her own.

It is, of course, quite possible that I had succumbed to the perennial temptation of ministers by conveying an impression of being so busy that she had not felt free to approach me. Her opening greeting, "I'd like [a visit], if you can spare the time," and the expression of gratitude near the end, "I certainly appreciate all the time you have taken," indicate the value she attaches to "time." It would probably be correct to infer from these remarks that she had not taken the initiative previously, mainly because of her tendency to shoulder her own burdens and refrain from "bothering" others. Obviously this is a reciprocal matter, not an either/or one. That is to say, a more relaxed attitude on my part, a going out of my way to drink a cup of tea with her, *might* have made it easier for her to seek help earlier. In any case, my subconscious feelings about prior claims clearly made for an unnecessarily categorized approach.

At the time of the visit, Mrs. Jackson clearly wanted me to relate to her as a pastor, and I felt comfortable with this. My general orientation was vaguely Rogerian. By this I mean both that I was somewhat aware of my own limited ability to put the client-centered approach in practice, and also that I was not prepared to "buy" Rogers' formulation as the final or universally applicable one (though I did not have a clear and systematic theory as to when to depart from it). Yet I did intend to try to convey positive regard for Mrs. Jackson, to hear how things looked and felt from her internal frame of reference, and to reflect my understanding of this.

In the dialogue itself, once or twice I was consciously able to resist my natural inclination to respond in other ways. I managed to refrain from asking what precisely her husband's new job was, in response to 16, and from seeking clarification of those comments in 22 about the teen-age daughter that I did not understand. Although these matters were part of the overall situation, her own feelings about this situation and her personal collapse seemed to be more important than such details.

In practice, however, what I had to say all too frequently reflected neither her significant feelings nor my own good intentions. Some of the early responses such as my question at 7 and the personal observation in 9 were typical of everyday conversational gambits, although fortunately they did not distract her from giving vent to her personal troubles. But some of my contributions were "unforgivable"—as generations of students have been quick to tell me. My interruption at 19 is perhaps the grossest example. Note that though I state in parentheses, "confused, and seeking to clarify," the phrasing of my remark makes it quite clear that I *had become* aware (if only a split second before) that I had been on the wrong track. Thus I had *no need* to request clarification—quite apart from the fact that my doing so had the effect of making her feel foolish! This was an almost reflexive expression of surprise on my part, as "natural" and as detrimental as the shocked look or uncontrolled gasp when someone blurts out the story of his incestuous practices.

Various other of my responses were poor or inadequate to one degree or another. At 25, for example, "You really have been overloaded with everything, and all the responsibility," manages to reflect an important *part* of what Mrs. Jackson has just said. But it fails to pick up and include her negative feelings about herself as one who has failed her children by default, in not getting them to church. Two other remarks also raise more general issues that will be further discussed in Chapter IV. Suffice it to note here that the minister's response at 31—"Yes. And *you* need to be able to share the burden at times"—is prescriptive, and is so on the basis of a presumed psychological competence rather than a specifically spiritual one.

My response at 15 is worth a closer look, too. Mrs. Jackson has just told me that it is hell living *in* a soap opera, but that things will be better now and the rest is doing her good, that I have been a great help, and that she hopes she'll be able to manage. The intention of my response to this is reality-testing, because she sounds overly optimistic to me. However, it fails to pick up her *ambivalent* feelings—she *hopes* things will be better, but isn't too sure that they will. Consequently it forces her into trying to marshal evidence to prove her point. But note that the other side of the coin—picking up only her *positive* feelings with some such response as, "Things look a little brighter now"—would have been little if any improvement. Only if both parts of a person's feelings, commonly of love *and* hate, are faithfully reflected, is he freed to take them seriously without undervaluing one and defending the other.

The responses that have been alluded to so far reveal relatively minor, or at least delimited, errors. But at two points in particular, I failed to convey adequate understanding of quite crucial feelings that Mrs. Jackson was vividly expressing, where to have done so might have helped her more. Underlying her remarks in 10 and her closing defense in 22, and explicit in 24 and 26, was the feeling that she had fallen short in her responsibilities. On later reflection, it seems probable that this woman has had unrealistic expectations of herself. Her repeated expression, "I've tried to play God too long," suggests that she had already gained some awareness of this. But a more reflective response on my part would probably have facilitated a deeper realization of the innate impossibility of such a role.

As it was, the minister's responses 13 and 27 are deficient in both form and content. Each of them is couched in very didactic and generalizing terms. And 13 in particular offers too many openings to be taken the wrong way. It could be heard, for example, as a rejection of her feelings, as (premature) reassurance, or even as implying that I don't really

care about Mrs. Jackson herself! It *does* seem from her re-
joinder in 14 that she picked up the intended contrast that
was the point of my long-winded statement. "Uh-huh, I see.
And it's like that for psychiatrists too, I suppose. [But] it certainly is hell living *in* a soap opera." But perhaps a brief reflection of what she was implying, such as, "It seems to you
that a minister's concern for his people is the same as your
feeling of responsibility for your family," might have given
her room to reject the analogy as fallacious for herself. However desirable a clarification of her dubious equation may
have been at the time, I was obviously too concerned to set
her right. And in any event, she was clearly willing to give up
the effort to communicate at this point. "Things will be better
now. . . . You've been a great help, . . . and I hope I'll be
able to manage," comes pretty close to "thank you and
good-by!"

The other serious failure was in connection with her vivid
remark, "It's hell living *in* a soap opera." Mrs. Jackson was
never really given a chance to develop or explore her intense
feelings in this connection.

Thus in summary, although the visit deepened our relationship, and was felt by Mrs. Jackson to have been of some help
(if this was anything more than mere politeness), it was not
nearly as effective as it could have been. The relationship
deepened principally, it would seem, because Mrs. Jackson
wanted to share her situation and feelings more fully than
ever before. This in turn seems to have been a consequence of
her having in some sense "reached the bottom," to use terminology normally applied to the alcoholic who finally admits
that he can't kick his drinking habit by himself. For Mrs.
Jackson here at least partly acknowledges her unavoidable
need for help. Given this urgency on her part, and the force-
fulness of her personality, she was able in fair measure to say
what she wanted to, despite the obstacles and digressions that
I introduced. Presumably some degree of my genuine concern

managed to communicate itself to Mrs. Jackson apart from what I actually said. For it has been shown that this element of concern on the part of the helping person is more basic and essential than any variation of technique.[6]

## PASTORAL THEOLOGY

Let us return to take another look at the same conversation between Mrs. Jackson and myself, but from a different perspective. What follows is a statement of what stands out in the encounter for me, looking at it in theological terms.

Please note that what is intended in this section is not an analysis of the chaplain's theology as revealed by his ministry. Such an understanding is quite feasible, and on occasion can be of considerable value, especially where it brings to light a discrepancy between a person's stated theology and that which he enacts. Competent supervision in clinical training would not fail to remark upon the dissonance of a stated conviction that "all have sinned and come short of the glory of God," when this goes hand in hand with self-righteousness of manner.

Another prefatory observation needs to be made. In this particular instance, as will appear, the theological analysis focuses on Mrs. Jackson and what she said. But in another encounter, something said by the minister, or revealed by the relationship—conflict, for example—might raise more crucial issues. Indeed, in the present case, others may legitimately discern the theological focus at a different point. As it happens, in another verbatim from which I have pursued extensive theological reflection, it was rather like Sherlock Holmes's case of "The Dog That Barked in the Night." The starting point for theological thinking[7] was behavior that did *not* take place, although it seemed strongly called for.

From the above conversation, the following remarks by Mrs. Jackson seem to me to be the most significant and fruitful for

theological reflection: (10) "I've tried to play God too long.
. . . Everyone in the family looks to me. And now I've had
to give in. I couldn't take it any longer. (14) Things will be
better now. This rest is certainly doing me good . . . and I
hope I'll be able to manage. (24) On top of everything else
I just haven't been able to see to it [i.e., getting the younger
children to Sunday school]. They are just little heathens, I
suppose. . . . (26) You see so many people worse off than
yourself . . . you feel that you ought to be able to carry on.
But I shouldn't have tried to play God so long. (30) Well I
certainly feel better since I gave up trying to do it all. . . .
(32) It has done me a lot of good to be able to share this. (34)
I feel I need a few more days rest before I can go back to face
it all."

What is revealed by these statements might appear to point
to a number of theological issues. For one thing, there is evidently a feeling of something like *guilt,* certainly for having
failed to meet her responsibilities, and perhaps also for having
unrealistically tried to do so alone. Alternatively, this emphasis on having to do everything and carry the whole burden
might be taken as indicating a *"works theology"* on her part.
Or again, a new *hope* might seem to be in the air, in her dawn-
ing realization that she is not alone and that support is available, together with some slight indications of greater readiness
on her part to accept such help. My own conclusion, however,
is that none of these possibilities precisely pins down the central issue. Mrs. Jackson does not seem to be so much burdened
by feelings of guilt, as accepting that she hasn't done all she
wanted to. There doesn't appear to be any clear indication
that by her efforts she is consciously striving to merit the love
and acceptance of God. And she was not so much unaware
that help was available before her hospitalization, as she was
intent on doing without it if she possibly could.

Neither do I believe that this is an open-and-shut case of a
woman who has done her best to cope with an increasingly

intolerable situation, and has finally collapsed under the strain. Undoubtedly, her situation is a rough one. It may have been so for a long time, inasmuch as her husband was hospitalized for alcoholism many years prior to this. But the inescapable question is: How much has Mrs. Jackson herself contributed to this? How *can* a family get into such a mess (in addition, the oldest daughter bore a child out of wedlock several years ago), unless the whole environment is unhealthy in some way? Furthermore, Mrs. Jackson is too intelligent and experienced not to have been able to recognize long before this that the situation was getting out of hand—unless she is driven by an unconscious need to hold the reins in her hands. Mrs. Jackson strikes me less as being driven by moral or religious precepts to fulfill all of her family's superabundant needs than as having *chosen* this role. Fundamentally, her self-concept appears to be of herself as the one who can be and is going to be the strong one in the family. (How far any deficiencies on the part of her husband reinforced this self-concept, and how far her style of life influenced his reactions to stress is unknown.) Yet at the same time, there is a noticeable ambivalence in Mrs. Jackson's feelings, perhaps recent in origin or at least strengthened by the present crisis. She feels that too much is expected of her, and she is becoming more willing to recognize her need for help as well as to accept help from others.

Thus, theologically, the underlying (though not the obtrusive) principle involved here appears to me to be *the tension inherent in responsible creaturehood.* That is to say, the central problem seems to be the innate one for mankind of balancing the necessary striving to become a self, a mature person in one's own right, with the givenness of being finite creatures who, willy-nilly, are dependent and limited.

It is most improbable that Mrs. Jackson would formulate her doctrinal beliefs in any terms that implied, let alone asserted, her ultimate self-dependence. Nevertheless, she has

been acting as if this were the case, and is now showing signs
of awareness that she has indeed been behaving in this way.
However, her ambivalence is showing. She admits that she has
gone on too long under her own steam alone, and has arro-
gated God's position to herself. She has come some way toward opening herself to the help of other human beings—
psychiatrist, minister, and chaplain—and voices the feeling
that this has been beneficial. She verbalizes recognition of the
fact that she was licked, and that she could not successfully
be completely self-dependent. Yet at the same time, she is still
expressing the feeling that she ought to have been able to cope
with the situation. She believes that she can get through even
the tough spots with the aid of laughter. The slight turn that
circumstances have taken for the better with her husband
finding employment prompts her to think that she may be able
to manage in the future. And she talks in terms of going back
to it all again, after a brief period of recuperation and a mini-
mum of pastoral aid.

Here is no gross example of arrogant pride,[8] let alone a
Promethean defiance of the gods. Nevertheless, there would
seem to be room for greater recognition by Mrs. Jackson that
none of us can be fully responsible for anyone else's life, and
that we are all fallible, finite children of God who yet can
relax, not to abandon moral effort and responsibility, but in
the recognition that *he* has the whole world in his hands. It is
my impression that a great deal of Christian theology has
strongly emphasized that "pride" is the very essence of sin,
and that man has to be confronted with his sinful pride and
urged to repent and humble himself before Jesus as Lord. At
this point I find myself, with surprise (because I had not discerned this to be the case from the pastoral analysis), coming
to the conclusion that Mrs. Jackson's basic spiritual need is to
be convicted of the implicit arrogance and irrationality involved in her impossible self-dependence and assumption of
total responsibility for her family.

Quite deliberately, I have made no attempt to refresh my understanding of the Christian tradition's formulated insights into "pride" at this point. Consequently, my reflections leave me with questions that will have to be taken up in Chapter V. For one thing, does *pride*, in its orthodox theological sense, connote grasping and pretence at both the perfection of God and the power of God? In Mrs. Jackson's case, the self-righteousness appears to be subdominant at the most. But she does try to exercise the *power* of God over her family, and wants to know, in effect, "How do you other gods manage?" (12). Another question is raised by the fact that, when "well," she would play God more wholeheartedly but never admit it; whereas in the present crisis, when she is unable to fulfill this self-appointed role and it is less pronounced, it becomes evident to her and even admissible. Third, my understanding of the dynamics of this kind of behavior is obviously deficient. I have thought that underlying a need to control—whether it be the life of one's family, or in only offering a perfect book for publication—is typically a fear of loss of control and overt inadequacy. Yet phenomenologically, I find Mrs. Jackson neither noticeably afraid (nor angry), nor markedly "ashamed" of her present lack of control. The final question raised by the whole situation is of the reciprocal interaction within the family context of those whose temptation is to be assertive and controlling with those whose predilection it is to be doormats!

To sum up this section, I am saying that correlating Mrs. Jackson's plight as I perceive it and the Christian tradition as I understand it, "pride" is the most accurate description. It should be noted that this is intended as a phenomenological description, not an apportionment of blame. (In fact, I would suspect that a great deal of her way of life is a result of the way she was brought up and learned to relate to the world.) The purpose of this theological analysis is twofold. The theoretical, doctrinal ramifications will be taken up in Chapter V. Meanwhile, it has an immediate, practical use. Simply to say that "all men are sinners" is not particularly helpful in attempting to minister to a particular person or family. Specific ills require specific, and different, remedies. And the forms or modes of an individual's expression of his sinfulness are no less relevant to the pastor's task than is careful diagnosis of his disease to the practice of medicine.

## IMPLICATIONS FOR MINISTRY

Now it is time to turn back to consider what I said in this conversation, and how a future ministry could have proceeded from here in the light of theological reflection. (Unfortunately, such reflection actually took place only in rudimentary form prior to subsequent conversations.) Granted that the theological analysis is quite personal, the primary point is its potential as a source of more adequate operating principles for me. For, like it or not, everyone has to work on the basis of some principles, however vague or explicit, psychological or theological, consistent or fluctuating. There is simply no way of avoiding this.

The thrust of my responses in the actual conversation would seem to vary considerably. I endeavor to accept and understand Mrs. Jackson's final collapse under the stress of her external situation (11), and my next remark implies that most people would react similarly if they had to face it twenty-four hours a day. My comment in 15 does implicitly question whether she is being realistic in expecting to regain control of the situation if there has been no change apart from her having had a short rest. On the other hand, 25 empathizes with her feeling that she has had all the responsibility, which just proved too much—without in any way challenging her erroneous and dangerous basic assumption. The minister in 27 does imply doubt as to whether what she is still half intent on trying to do can be done within the terms she envisages, namely, a little more moral support from outsiders. However, my 29 and 31 make it explicit that such help is available if she decides to go ahead and try it. And my 35, in closing, is a rank assumption that nothing much *is* going to change. Moreover, my apparently going along with her intentions as right and proper is only minimally guarded by stress that more than physical health is needed. In sum, there is almost nothing in what I said to Mrs. Jackson that would lead her to think more deeply about her basic presuppositions, which seem on theological analysis to be one of the major roots of her troubles. Indeed more often than not she receives at least implicit support for her efforts and intentions.

In the light of the theological analysis, the contrast between what was done and what needs to be done is unmistakable. It becomes clear that my future procedures should not be directed toward reassuring Mrs. Jackson that she has done a very creditable job, and is a pillar of church and home who can be justly proud of the way all her family look to her and lean upon her. This would be to lend her pride the support of formal ecclesiastical approval! Nor, at the other extreme, would accusation and direct confrontation be likely to help, inasmuch as it usually produces an effect diametrically opposite to that desired.

Just as a belief in the reality of forgiveness is sometimes a prerequisite to the very possibility of repentance,[9] so this woman must be enabled to recognize and abandon her impossible aspirations in a manner that does not lead her to react too defensively. For in this particular case, Mrs. Jackson's psychic bondage and her broken, or at least impaired, relationship with God would seem to be inextricably bound together.[10] (That Mrs. Jackson's relationship with God is impaired is being inferred on the basis of her symptoms of prideful sin. Although there was testimony concerning religious behavior in the conversations, she did not elaborate on her faith itself. She sees herself as having played God. The implications of this for her actual concept of God stagger the imagination. He must be an overworked and probably overextended managing director of The World, Inc.)

It would thus seem theoretically possible to proceed in this relationship in either of two ways, according to the opportunities offered. On the one hand, Mrs. Jackson might be enabled in practical terms to move toward a less all-consuming feeling of total responsibility for her family, so that she is neither involved to the point of physical breakdown herself, nor overwhelmed with a feeling of failure at their breakdowns. A move toward greater health would be the explicit result. But a potentially more accurate understanding of her creaturehood before God would be implicit, and might dawn on her.

Alternatively, it might be possible to help her toward an acceptance of the fact that, finally, she can only be answerable for herself before God, and even so, only as a justified sinner. In this eventuality, she would consciously be moving with the help of grace toward a more satisfactory relationship with God. But along with this she would almost inevitably improve in "health" as a consequence of the more relaxed attitude toward her family that this redemptive process would entail.

In either case, it would have to become apparent to Mrs. Jackson that she can rely on my support and acceptance rather than having to "do it all herself." Then, I should hope, she might be able to relax the reins somewhat, and let the members of her family be responsible for themselves. In addition to genuinely embodying concern and trustworthiness and support, I could perhaps best achieve this by more carefully reflecting any further statements to the effect that she "ought" to be able to do everything, and that she is going back to take up the intolerable burden again. If the relationship is reasonably adequate, she might be able to risk facing deeper consideration of what such statements imply.

The main point of this section, then, has been to demonstrate that in my opinion I arrived at a more satisfying and helpful understanding of what was going on in this ministry by thinking about it in theological terms. The reader will notice that I *now* think that the crucial feelings needing reflection are, not the self-pity with undertones of anger at the hellish soap opera in which she is living, nor even the feeling of failure at having fallen short in her responsibilities, but precisely the categorical imperatives that Mrs. Jackson imposes on herself, as to what she ought to have done and ought not to have done.

The charge of spiritual pride may be leveled at me, too, for the presumptuous attempt to analyze Mrs. Jackson. I have not meant to convey an Olympian attitude of looking down on the situation of mere mortals. But, for a sinful man, this is always possible. I can only reassert that we *do* all minister on the basis of our appraisals of situations, whether these be made systematically or on hunches, so that this risk is never absent.

## FOLLOW-UP

Five days later, I visited Mrs. Jackson again. Only a very embryonic version of the foregoing analysis had taken place. The part of the conversation that I wrote up afterward went, after some introductory remarks, as follows:

*Mrs. J.:*   36   And things should be better now that I have a new perspective. At least I think, I hope, I pray they will.

*Minister:*   37   May I ask what this new perspective is, that you have arrived at?

*Mrs. J.:*   38   Well, it comes in two parts. First, there is my job. I may have told you that when I came here several years ago, it was completely unstructured. And of course when that is the case, it can be worse than having a set number of hours and set tasks. And everything seems expected of me. I've sent the director [administrator] a note, to talk it over. One gets fed up of being treated like a child! And when you're depressed, it doesn't help to be taken into that office and hauled over the coals. You don't feel up to it. But he thinks my family is interfering with my job. It doesn't matter to him that the job is as well done as anywhere in the county. That's how he's going to have it. He said it would be no trouble to get someone else if I couldn't do it. And that hurt. And I'm not sure that he could, that easily.

*Minister:*   39   But I gather that you don't want to give up the job if you can avoid it.

*Mrs. J.:*   40   By no means. I enjoy it. But I'm on call twenty-four hours a day, you know. And a little while back there was one of the staff who thought I ought to be available for every little question, and he would go stamping in to the director, and he would phone me and then haul me over the carpet. But if I'm supposed to be a department head, then there should be coverage and an adequate staff for the job—but it gets treated as if anyone at all could do it. In actual fact I've hardly taken any time off at all . . . (*She went on to document this in detail.*) So anyway, the director phoned the psychiatrist to ask when I would be back to work, but he didn't get much change out of him. (*Then followed some comments about her respect for the director, nonetheless. She mentioned his Scottish stubbornness; yet how one morning after he had made an "irrevocable decision" against her advice, he had come in first thing to admit that she had been right; and how she thinks he respects her as she does him.*) So I sent him this little note, to talk things over.

Minister:    41    And if you don't get *any* reasonable compromise or satisfaction, you would reluctantly feel that you had to give up the job.

Mrs. J.:    42    Yes. I hope it isn't necessary—but it would be ridiculous to go on like this. I'd be back in here. And it might be worse next time. . . . (*Mrs. Jackson continues.*) My middle daughter has got to learn to care about herself. She doesn't at the moment. She gives herself out to everyone.

Minister:    43    You see something of the same pattern in her that you do in yourself.

Mrs. J.:    44    Yes, she resembles me a lot in some ways. She had written eight novels by the time she was seventeen. . . . But she has to learn to look out for her own development and see herself as a person. . . . (*Mrs. Jackson concludes:*) Secondly, I've got to learn that I can't do everything. The family has made use of me—exploited me, in fact. They are managing all right while I am not there. But when I am there, they treat it as a job, and don't think of me as a person. When I leave here I am going to spend a fortnight or so with my sister-in-law. And they are just going to have to get used to not having me around to do everything. . . . That prayer attributed to St. Francis has a lot of meaning for me. I can't remember it exactly, but about changing what ought to be changed and leaving what can't, and "grant me the wisdom to distinguish the one from the other." This is the hard thing, and where I've erred. I am learning not to think "I must, must, *must* do this or that." This week has been really valuable, in realizing that I need help. I've always avoided it if I possibly could. My husband at least is beginning to realize—whereas he used to be wrapped up in his own problems.

We tied all this together with thinking about the need to recognize that, while we have some responsibility toward others, we cannot be totally responsible for them, because ultimately each person must answer to God for himself. Mrs. Jackson had also mentioned with real appreciation her priest's steadfast concern and regular visits, and also the steps he was taking to help the middle daughter.

I visited Mrs. Jackson a few more times before she was discharged, but regrettably did not write up the conversations.

# II

## MRS. JACKSON—MAY

### INTRODUCTION

On visiting a member of the congregation who was in the hospital, I discovered that Mrs. Jackson had been readmitted the previous day with a diagnosis of "acute depressive reaction." (I had seen her only once in the interval since our conversations in January, as she had been on extended sick leave. She had been visiting her husband in the hospital in March, and despite having a bad dose of flu, was looking somewhat improved.)

Visits on that day and two days later revealed that she had left her sister-in-law's to spend four days at home over the Easter holiday, "and this was enough to set me right back." She voiced the feeling that her family had not changed at all, and that they let her slave for them all around the clock while they slept, watched "telly" (television), or went out. She expressed increasing doubts about the likelihood of her ever returning to work. And she said that her greatest worry was for Barbara (twelve years) and David (eleven years), and the effect all this was having on them.

A third visit found her in the depths of depression. She had learned over the weekend that her oldest daughter had forged her signature to a check for £25 on her personal account. (The girl had permission to sign checks on the parents' joint account temporarily because Mr. Jackson was too shaky to hold a pen and Mrs. Jackson was in the hospital.) I ventured to wonder with her whether—with the two youngest being taken care of by relatives, and Lily by another relative—the only possible future with a prospect of health and emotional stability for Mrs. Jackson might not be one apart from her family for the time being, and perhaps with a routine kind of job until she got back on her feet. Verbally, at least, she did not rule this out as a possibility—which is some indication of her desperation. If one were unwary, it might even be taken as a sign of positive movement, but for having noted the yo-yo-like fluctuation of her attitudes.

Two days later found Mrs. Jackson appearing a little more lively. But it had been a big shock to her to find out that her husband had been brought into the hospital quite seriously ill with a reaction to the drugs he had been taking. She herself was getting electric shock treatments at this time. After this visit, I resolved to be disciplined in writing up all future conversations with this family. It was becoming obvious that the whole situation over an extended period was both volatile and serious, however unspectacular any particular pastoral visit might seem.

### CONVERSATION

| | | |
|---|---|---|
| *Minister:* | 45 | (*I knock on the door, for, being a member of the staff, Mrs. Jackson was in a side room off the ward, and she always kept her door shut.*) May I come in? |
| *Mrs. J.:* | 46 | Yes, do. You must be glad to get in out of the weather. I went along to see Mr. Jackson last night. (*I had passed on a request from him that she would do so, since he was confined* |

*to bed himself the previous day.*) I don't like parading up and down the corridor, but under the circumstances!

Minister: 47 I remember your saying so. I've been along to see him twice this morning, but he was sleeping each time.

Mrs. J.: 48 Last night I felt up to going. But today I haven't been able. I have a treatment this morning, and have another one tomorrow, and I still feel a little muzzy. Thank heavens for aspirin! They [the electroshock treatments] leave you with such a frightful headache.

Minister: 49 (*Thinking she was hinting that she still had a headache*) Would you rather I came back and visited you somewhat later?

Mrs. J.: 50 Oh, no. I'm all right now. They have the aspirin here about the time I'm waking up. Only this morning they forgot to bring the drinking water. I'll get the nurse to fetch some when she comes for my tray.

Minister: 51 (*Seeing this not as switching away from her, since it is so much a part of her situation*) How did you think your husband was when you saw him last night?

Mrs. J.: 52 Not too bad. He was coherent. But he looked awfully washed out, as if he'd really been through the mill. (*In a brief and somewhat detached manner*) It is quite an amazing thing, especially when the pharmaceutical company claims that these things have no side effects!

Minister: 53 Presumably they mean, "no side effects when taken as prescribed?" (*Arguing, purposeless and unjustified!*)

Mrs. J.: 54 Yes. And I don't know how many Jack has

been taking. He has been relying on them too long. Dr. Singh has taken a sample and sent it to the pharmaceutical company which puts the drug on the market.

*Minister:*   55   You mean a sample of his blood? (!)

*Mrs. J.:*   56   I suppose so. It is not the drug alone, but I never know what might happen. Apparently the drug will produce its own hangover, but with quite a moderate amount of alcohol the effect is boosted enormously. That's what happened to a friend of mine. She was a widow with three children to bring up, and very good at her job. But when they left home she began drinking more and more. Once she was brought in in convulsions—and very soon she was dead. She wasn't very old either. So I became quite worried, and talked to the psychiatrist about it. And he and Dr. Singh sat down together, and so Dr. Singh took him off all drugs. (*Pause.*) I feel better every day— at least, I think so. But I don't know what's going to happen. I have up to six months' sick leave, but I don't know whether I will be able to come back at all. Just between you and me, I don't know whether they will want me back, or whether Miss Graham [the temporary replacement] will have done such a good job that they won't. But it would have to be less strain in any case. Everyone tells me that I have tried to do too much and will have to ease off.

*Minister:*   57   What do you think that might mean in practical terms for the future?

*Mrs. J.:*   58   I just don't know. I thought I was getting on fine, and then everything just sort of became a—a . . .

| *Minister:* | 59 | Everything fell down around you. |
|---|---|---|
| *Mrs. J.:* | 60 | That's exactly right. And now Jack is back in the hospital again too. It was about ten years ago when the shipyards started to contract and lay men off that he began to rely on tranquilizers. He had an excellent job, and was to have been made head of his department when his boss retired—and then the department began to be shut down! His boss retired three years ago, which was a year early. And Jack would have taken over. |
| *Minister:* | 61 | (*Deliberately fishing—both the objective origins of this situation and her perception of them seem to be important.*) So his problem just dates back to ten years ago? |
| *Mrs. J.:* | 62 | Yes. I've coddled him since he broke his back last year, and tried not to press him. But sometimes he would go into what I used to call, when I got really fed up, a mid-Victorian decline. You know: Just took to his bed, and you could do nothing with him. And for seven days at a time—so that he couldn't have been going out and buying booze. It must have been the drugs. But now he's got to learn that he can't depend on pills to solve all his problems. As somebody once said, there's no pill for pills! But relatives have taken the younger children, and that's a great relief. |
| *Minister:* | 63 | You can at least be sure that they are being taken care of. |
| *Mrs. J.:* | 64 | Yes, I can. And a friend in town has the older girls for the time being. Only I told her to tell them to see to the cat and dog. It's too cold for them to go out this weather. Between you and me, I don't know what's going to happen about the job. Of course, it |

may be that Miss Graham is doing a better
job than me. I don't believe it though. I know
her, and her experience doesn't compare with
mine. She's a good occupational therapist, but
she's never been responsible for planning the
whole program for a hospital and running it.
So I'll have to go back and beard the lion
[the hospital director] in his den. As I say, I
have up to six months, and I may take all of
that. At first I fondly thought I'd be back in a
couple of months.

But it'll have to be different. I couldn't
stand all the strain and tensions of before. In
the nine years I've been here some of the
other departments have multiplied by three
and four in staff—and the number of patients
has more than doubled. And I just can't do it.
Even some secretarial assistance with all the
government forms and red tape would help.
But the boss doesn't understand.

But I could always go back to my original
love—painting, you know. I've had water-
colors shown, not just here, but in London.
And I've got a number of canvases that I've
been working on in oils. I could do it. But
who's interested in art galleries these days?
They all sit glued to the goggle box. Oh, I
watch it sometimes, for the documentaries,
and factual reports on BBC, and Wimbledon
—but not all the stuff they have on the independent channel. I get unpopular with the
children because I switch it off at home. It
stunts people's imaginations.

But thank heavens for my friends at a time
like this.

*Minister:* 65 They've really come through now that you need them.

*Mrs. J.:* 66 Yes, they have. And you know that I don't like to rely on other people. But in a way it has taken this to find out just how many friends I had. Yet where do I go from here? Every time I feel better, the family knocks me down again. The whole thing's a mess.

*Minister:* 67 There doesn't seem to be anything stable, as a jumping-off point.

*Mrs. J.:* 68 No, there doesn't. It's not really big things, but the repeated troubles. If only I could see a little bit of blue sky.

*Minister:* 69 Everything is confused at once. Whereas if Mr. Jackson, say, were O.K., you could work from there. But as it is, all the troubles reinforce one another.

*Mrs. J.:* 70 Yes. Like, when my father died, well, it was a big shock. But after a bit it subsided, and we all carried on.

*Minister:* 71 Everything else was stable, and you could make a fresh start on the basis of that. Whereas now it's like a muddy bog, with no firm footing at all.

*Mrs. J.:* 72 That's exactly it. Everything is unstable. But Jack ought to be able to get a good job with Funboats Incorporated. He was one of their first draftsmen, you know, thirty years ago. And with all his experience of marine engineering, he ought to be very valuable. And he's not an introvert. At least, he's not as introverted as I am. He has no hesitation in bearding those lions in their dens. Janet [the oldest daughter] ought to be back in the university this year. And Lily ought to go next year. She's too bright to miss it. Everything couldn't have happened at a worse time. (*But she began to go back over old ground again, and I made my departure, promising to return in a couple of days.*)

I checked with Mrs. Jackson's boss, the hospital director, before I left the hospital. We had talked in professional confidence about the situation before, when I had felt it necessary to be sure I understood the objective situation regarding her job. He himself had checked with the psychiatrist, who had said that he felt there was no real likelihood of her being up to it. Moreover, the replacement, Miss Graham, who came on very short notice, was doing a good job. (The hospital director also passed on a rumor that he had heard from one of the staff as to the original crisis that had triggered off this whole convoluted mess, but said that he had no way of knowing whether or not there was any truth in it.)

The flow of her talk was much more nonstop today. Except for the brief reflective statements noted, I had nothing to do apart from nodding encouragingly. It is noticeable that unlike the main verbatim in the previous chapter (1–35), she did not put me on the spot with direct questions.

My own overall reading of the situation is that there is yet a great need for her to make a radical revision downward of her perceptions regarding the abilities and future prospects of both her husband and herself. The very possibility of an emotionally stable future for her may depend on an extended period away from the rest of the family, but there is the obvious danger with this kind of action that her feeling of "failure," if not of guilt at leaving even her husband and adult daughter to fend for themselves might more than offset the advantages. It would also seem probable that she is going to have to think in terms of a relatively routine occupation without great responsibilities, if she intends to seek full-time employment. And if she does not, she will have to think of her painting as a re-creating hobby rather than a pathway to fame and fortune.

The problem for me becomes that of whether I have the right to attempt any appraisal of the situation with her, and if so when and how.

FURTHER CONVERSATIONS

Two days later I stopped by to see Mrs. Jackson again.

*Mrs. J.:*  73  Come in.

*Minister:*  74  You're not trying to sleep?

*Mrs. J.:*  75  No, not yet. I'm feeling much better, more relaxed. Everyone says I'm looking better. (*I couldn't see this—but did not say so!*) I should have done this a long time ago. I don't know how it will be when I get back to all the tension though.

*Minister:*  76  You feel fine here in the peace of the hospital, but obviously you're just not sure how long it will last under fire.

*Mrs. J.:*  77  No, I'm not. Easter was such a flop. The older girls are at an age when they are courting now, and they would be out. And the poison must have been building up in my husband's weak system even then. Otherwise he would at least have noticed. (*She went back over there not being even a clean sheet for her bed, since everything had just been stuffed away in the drawers, clean and dirty together. And she elaborated on some of Lily's escapades, finishing,* "but I don't let it get me upset anymore.")

> The Father has been extremely good, in arranging for the children to stay with families in the congregation who have kids the same age.
>
> I should have done this [i.e., come into the hospital as a patient] long before, but I was prejudiced, I suppose [i.e., against E.S.T.]. Father Dawson said that everyone is prejudiced against something, but I have trained myself to be open-minded. (*Here Mrs. Jackson elaborated on past examples.*)

At this point a friend came in to visit her, and after a few pleasantries I left. As I was departing, she was again saying how well she felt, and remarked: "The doctor even says I'm getting my sense of humor back, and that's a sure sign."

This was an abortive twenty-minute visit, with the interruption anyway. There was some new background material concerning her early married life. There were also incipient signs of returning (over-) confidence as a result of a slight improvement in her feelings and a (temporary only) amelioration of her situation.

The following conversation, which lasted for a little over thirty minutes, took place three days later. Mr. Jackson was present in his wife's room for the first part of it.

| | | |
|---|---|---|
| *Minister:* | 78 | I thought I might find you here, too, Mr. Jackson. How are you both getting on? |
| *Mr. J.:* | 79 | Only fair. I had an E.E.G. [electroencephalogram] today, and start E.S.T. tomorrow. |
| *Mrs. J.:* | 80 | (*Starting from the shawl she was wearing, borrowed from a friend, Mrs. Jackson launched into a discussion of shawls and woolens in general. When that was exhausted, I tried to bring Mr. Jackson into the conversation.*) |

| *Minister:* | 81 | Your wife was telling me, Mr. Jackson, that you worked for the Funboats Company in the early days. (*I chose the subject of work deliberately, because of the need for him to consider various employment possibilities for the future.*) |
|---|---|---|
| *Mr. J.:* | 82 | Yes. It wasmy first job after I left school. |
| *Mrs. J.:* | 83 | Yes. It was my first job after I left school. men, weren't you? |
| *Mr. J.:* | 84 | Yeah. |
| *Minister:* | 85 | What sort of work did it involve? |
| *Mr. J.:* | 86 | Motorboat construction. They were just beginning the firm in those days. |
| *Minister:* | 87 | And you helped design them? |
| *Mr. J.:* | 88 | Yes. Of course, they're all fiberglass now. (*Pause.*) I wish this clay would dry. I can't get it off. They have to put it on to attach the electrodes apparently. They say it'll come off when it dries, so I suppose I'll just have to wait. |
| *Mrs. J.:* | 89 | Father Dawson has been so good to us. Relatives have had our two younger children, you know, but they're rather old and so it's a bit much for them. And Father Dawson has organized it all within the parish for them to stay with a family. It'll be much nicer for them to stay with children their own age anyway. I've never known such a worker for getting things done. Our relatives were very impressed. He was in here last night when Lily arrived. And she said straight out—she'd been at church that morning—"Your sermon was too long." And he said, "Yes, it was." All the churches are preaching on the same thing, Acts. It's Reformation Sunday, and the same text in all the churches. Last year it was |

Ephesians, wasn't it, Jack? ["Yes," *said Mr. Jackson.*] And this year it's from Acts.

Mr. J.:    90    Well, I think I'll go along to my room. I still feel pretty wobbly.

Mrs. J.:    91    (*As he walked out in his hospital gown*) You're a fine figure of a man.

Mr. J.:    92    Yes, aren't I.

Minister:    93    I'll be in again on Wednesday, Mr. Jackson, and I'll come see you then.

Mr. J.:    94    Yes, please do. (*Exit.*)

Mrs. J.:    95    I hope the E.S.T. will help him out of his depression. And he can get back on his feet. The doctor said that I get my last E.S.T. tomorrow, and will probably get out of here on Wednesday.

Minister:    96    Yes. Will you go to your relatives?

Mrs. J.:    97    Yes, at first. And then as soon as I feel like it, I'll go to London. We've got a standing invitation there. Do you know the Lloyds? (*I replied that I did not know them.*) They're fine people . . . (*another couple of minutes about that family*).

Minister:    98    (*As that was exhausted, and feeling that it might be a good time to get the history in perspective*) How did Mr. Jackson come to leave Funboats?

Mrs. J.:    99    He got a good offer from one of the Tyne shipyards, with a big step up. Then he went into the navy (*no details offered*). After the war was over, he had a lot of offers. He had the contacts. John Peterson, you know. (*I said I did not know him.*) Oh, he was the one who gave Blanton House to the National Trust. But both of us felt after the navy it would be best to take the least high-pressure job. (*Why?*) And so there was this small Tyne shipyard, which looked as if it would be [suitable]. And his prospects there were excellent. He would have been head of his department by now. And then it began to fold up under him. (*Full details regarding some management decisions, one made contrary to Mr. Jackson's advice, which had turned out to the firm's detriment.*) That was awfully hard on Jack.

*Minister:* 100    It must have been, especially coming prematurely like that. I suppose all of us have to pull in our horns around retirement, and in some jobs a man may know that he's not going to get any promotion after about fifty. But to have the whole thing collapse and leave him out of a job so early must have been devastating.

*Mrs. J.:* 101    Yes, and this was four years ago. So he was under fifty at the time.

At first he hadn't really settled there, and would have looked for a change. But the prospects looked so good. And he knew (*not, "was told"*) he would become a department head. It was so secure and so I persuaded him to stay, and he agreed. After all, we had two young children then. The other two weren't born, of course. (*This feeling that she had urged the staying may be incorrect, and in any case it was very low key. But if it was accurately heard, the dynamic repercussions at the time of the firm's collapse may have been considerable.*) Now if he could just get back to some work.

I'm beginning to feel much better, and

ready to tackle the job again, if I get some help. Other departments have help. And it's just too much. It is bad enough even for a single woman, or a woman without children (*her successor is unmarried*). When I came, the children were much younger, and it was left to me to work the time out as I could. Miss Jenkins in Physiotherapy has assistants and clerical help, too. And even Jane Smith has Mrs. Knowles to back her up. I started this department, you know. Oh, well, we'll just have to wait and see what the future brings.

*Minister:* 102 Perhaps the future doesn't "bring" anything specifically, but you have to come to terms with the future.

*Mrs. J.:* 103 Well, as long as Jack can find some constructive work, at which he could be happy. It's tough for a man not to be able to support his family.

*Minister:* 104 Is it possible that work can be "constructive" in two different senses? The work itself may be constructive—but you and I know that in our society Mr. Jackson doesn't stand a very good chance of being wanted for something like that when he is over fifty. Or the work, as a clerk, say, may be very routine—but enable a man to bring home £800 a year and at least be the basic support of his family, and so be extremely constructive in that sense.

*Mrs. J.:* 105 Yes, that is so. I hope the E.S.T. will help Mr. Jackson to get out of his depression pattern. We want to see the children through the university. Lily ought to be able to get into North Staffs this fall. Janet (the oldest) muffed her chance. But then there will be Barbara and David to get through. (*Mrs. Jackson quite ignores the fact that county grants are graduated according to parents' income, and that children from poor families get through without any parental help at all.*) And I'd like to get well enough to get on with my painting. I've done quite a lot of creative work, you know. And I've an oil I want to do before I come back to work, for the show next month. In fact, if it is well received, I might not need to come back at all! My doctor has led me to hope (?) that I'll be able to manage. But it depends if the hospital will face the facts. I just couldn't do the fifty-hour week anymore.

*Minister:* 106 And if they wouldn't alter the situation, you would in fact have no option.

*Mrs. J.:* 107 That's right. But maybe they want someone to take charge of the home occupational therapy program. Mrs. Shiel is sort of doing the job now, and has some experience. But she doesn't have anything like the experience I have. Well, I suppose I'll have to wait and see.

*Minister:* 108 Well, Mrs. Jackson, you said you'll be going home on Wednesday, so this will be the last visit from me—though I'll keep visiting your husband, of course. And I hope the next time I see you, you will be back on your feet with your old zest for living. Meanwhile I will be thinking of you and praying for you.

Her discharge being delayed for a couple of days, there was in fact a further visit. However, not only was Mr. Jackson present, but also a friend of Mrs. Jackson's. This lady had had some travel experiences in common with mine, which Mrs. Jackson deliberately brought up for us to share impressions. This ruled out anything but a social visit.

## PASTORAL CARE

By this point Mrs. Jackson seems less of a stranger, even to someone just reading the conversations. Various elements of the pattern of her personality and her modes of discourse are beginning to stand out. For instance, it is becoming increasingly evident that despite the constant flow of words, most of her conversation is descriptive of the externals of her situation rather than expressive of her feelings about it. Even the infrequent instances of the latter are voiced in a very matter-of-fact tone. (I am not sure whether this is a mark of "good breeding" or simply an effect of medication.) This sharply raises the question of how one can best respond to the person who talks—steadily and copiously (and sometimes more tediously than in this case)—about her circumstances and feelings, substantiated with details, illustrations, and anecdotes, and often with a vivid turn of phrase, yet does not seem to think deeply about these things or to reveal much feeling at all!

More than in January, too, Mrs. Jackson seems to accept little responsibility for her own collapse. The frank acknowledgment of having tried to play God does not reappear, although this may follow naturally from her having been living apart from her family for most of the intervening months. But she attributes her problems to external sources—the family being so dependent upon her, the unfair demands of her job, her husband's problems with drink, drugs, and unemployment, and the unchanged attitudes at the Easter reunion. And she appears to be waiting for the environment, at home and at work, to change before she will be willing and able to cope. Superficially, she is blaming everyone else. But it is difficult to know whether at a deeper level she may not feel that she is the one who has failed and is to blame, but that this is too much to face up to. If this is indeed the case, it would seem to fit in with Gaylin's contention that "loss of self-confidence" is the essence of depression.[11]

For the first time, too, we are privileged to be participant observers while Mr. and Mrs. Jackson relate to one another! Of course they are both feeling below par, and that must be allowed for. But for all that, Mrs. Jackson sounds rather detached in her reaction (52) to her husband's hospitalization—much more so than is really required by the traditional British stiff upper lip. When they actually get together, he is quite self-absorbed and uncommunicative. She tries to draw him out in 83, following his brief response to me. But she does so by feeding him a question to which she already knows the answer, in fact treating him rather like a child and again he can answer with a terse "yeah." Just a minute or so later (insofar as my memory can be trusted as accurately recording the flow of the conversation), she entirely bypasses his grumbling expression of discomfort and changes the subject. And her parting shot as he takes his leave (in front of a third person) is less than kind, even though he covered any hurt by hamming it up and prancing out of the room.

My own conversational technique might be described as ranging from the sublime to the "gorblimey," except that it never reached the sublime! There is a sprinkling of questions —about her appraisal of her husband's condition (51), the onset of his problem (61), and his work history (98), as well as about her concrete estimate of what the future may hold for her (57), and her own immediate plans (96). There were silly interjections such as 53 and 55 that could have been actually harmful. My awful exit lines in 108 and in 35 in the previous chapter, perhaps saved on other occasions only by the arrival of visitors, suggest that this is an element of visiting which I need to work at improving. A brief summary of the ground that has been covered, for example, would be much better than "signing off" by responding solely to the last comment plus unwarranted optimism about the future. And in 100 and the two following comments, I am beginning to dig my heels in as she shows renewed signs of wanting the world to change to suit her. I resist her wishful thinking, and she, with equal tenacity, resists my attempt to intrude with harsh realities.

Others of my responses were of a more reflective manner. In 63 and 65 it was the desperation measure of reflecting the last sentence she had uttered. Following such a torrent of material, it is probably impossible to get gathered together in a brief sentence or two all that she has expressed, but it would be more helpful to pick up the salient clause rather than merely the final one. Indeed 65, although it is close enough to her frame of reference, is not strictly a reflection of her feelings at all, but an inference on the basis of what she has just said. "You feel very grateful for your friends" is what was needed. Similarly, in 59 I reflect her perception of the situation, whereas some such response as "you feel overwhelmed, or submerged" would have caught up her feelings directly. The last three contributions in that interview (67, 69, and 71), although primarily focused on the content of what she was expressing, would seem to have been genuinely reflective ones. And on the next visit a most promising start was made in 76, even catching the ambivalence she has expressed, before the pastoral conversation was aborted by the arrival of a visitor. (I can't help wondering how the idea got around that Rogerian reflection was an *easy* thing to do. It certainly isn't for me, as hardly needs stating, nor do others seem to find it so.)

This *goulash*—in terms of the variety of kinds of response I threw at Mrs. Jackson—raises an important issue that will have to be explored further in Chapter IV: that of the importance of *consistency* in the type of response made by a counselor.

In the first of these recorded visits, at least, Mrs. Jackson does seem to be a little more realistic about the future prospects with regard to her job (56 and 64). She has six months' sick leave, but is doubtful if she will be able to manage even after that. It is apparent to her that her original expectations of being back in her office after a few weeks' rest were unrealistically high. In the strictest confidence, she even shares her vague apprehension that the powers that be may not want her back because her replacement might be doing an adequate, equal, or even better job. She can't permit herself to believe that the latter could really be true, but she has come some way in even considering it as a hypothetical possibility. If she does come back to the same work, she would like the conditions to be different, and would press the hospital secretary for changes. There is little doubt that she would—and equally little doubt that the kind of changes she envisages will not occur. Whether she would actually take the job, supposing she had the chance, under the old conditions, remains an open question. But that there should be any question may in itself be a gain.

However, this may not be such a hopeful sign as it would appear to be if taken at face value. For closer inspection of the extended series of conversations makes clear that the current circumstances and situation exercise an inordinately strong influence on her feelings and attitudes. When she is feeling poorly, or betrayed, or freshly disappointed, she is ready to admit the magnitude of the problems, at least verbally. But the moment she begins to feel a little more "chipper," or when some faint glimmer of improvement in the external situation makes its presence felt there are immediate signs of returning overconfidence. For all the limitations on my part, and for all the chaos and crisis, Mrs. Jackson may not yet be ready to begin an examination of her feelings in relation to the situation in which she finds herself.

Another significant and rather subtle issue concerns the factors influencing my own fluctuating approach. The introduction to the series of conversations in this chapter mentions, alas without verbatim documentation of the context and form, my taking the initiative in raising an additional possible alternative future course of action for Mrs. Jackson. The point is that the suggested possibility is not a clear matter of pastoral competence. (This issue is taken up in the last section of Chapter IV.) It was based on a general awareness of psychiatric evidence. Apparently, remaining single is for some people a necessary condition of emotional stability, just as some people who can function adequately as a marital partner may find that the extra strain caused by the arrival of children pushes them to the breaking point.[12] By extension, then, it seemed possible that someone who had previously been able to cope with being a wife and a mother might no longer be able to do so, at least for the time being.

But this was in any case a very bold, if not brash, suggestion to make, however viable it may be in principle. Presumably, like my leading Mrs. Jackson into discussing her husband's situation, which I had avoided in January, it was also influenced by my (at that point rudimentary) analysis of earlier conversations. Yet my final comment in the appraisal indicates clearly that it was not done on the basis of a systematic new theory.

In addition to general knowledge from study of the literature of pastoral care and conscious or subconscious carry-over of previous impressions of Mrs. Jackson and her needs, a third source of "understanding" that may have influenced my approach to some degree was my conversations with the hospital secretary. From this source I had a secondhand report of the psychiatrist's prognosis, and a firsthand estimate of the ability of and satisfaction being given by Mrs. Jackson's replacement.

I thus had "objective knowledge" both that Mrs. Jackson was unlikely to get well enough to be able to return to her former job, and that she was not wanted back at the price of a lot of concessions.

Thus I risked the possibility of carrying over moods and experiences from one visit to another. (One thinks of Semelweiss, who used to haunt the hospital corridors in Vienna in the nineteenth century and *beg* the doctors not to go straight from the morgue to the maternity ward without at least washing their hands first.) But the analogy is too simple. Several kinds of carry-over were operative here. And there was the acute problem of an urgent desire on my part to "warn" Mrs. Jackson when she started getting too optimistic!

### PASTORAL THEOLOGY

From the tangled threads of this composite tapestry, a few are again selected for further reflection. The focus will be on those of Mrs. Jackson's attitudes ranging—without prejudice to their final analysis and labeling—from pessimism to optimism. The intent is to leave comparison with systematic theological descriptions of hope and despair until Chapter V. However it may be more difficult to avoid their intrusion at this point, since my own reading in this area has been of more recent date than was the case with respect to "pride." Consideration of Mr. Jackson's plight will be deferred until the next chapter, of which he is the central figure.

Mrs. Jackson's situation is truly chaotic. In addition to the mess revealed in Chapter I, her husband is back in the hospital with drug intoxication, her oldest daughter has indulged in forgery in order to steal from her parents while they are incapacitated, and four days at home over Easter have been enough to set Mrs. Jackson herself right back. Behind it all there is now lurking a rumor as to the precipitating factor that triggered the explosion!

The chaos threatens Mrs. Jackson with utter despair (66–72). There is *no* sure foothold left. Everything has fallen down around her at once, or does so repeatedly. To switch the metaphor, Mrs. Jackson finds herself all at sea, with not a solitary rock that she can recognize to grab hold of. Moreover, every time she gets back on her feet she is knocked down again by the breakers. Her cry is, where is she to start amid such total upheaval.

For all that, however, it is not clear that Mrs. Jackson has genuinely "reached bottom" in the alcoholic's or prodigal son's sense of *giving up* and acknowledging her inescapable need of help. She can *see* the bottom—it is close enough to be staring her in the face! Yet she is still asking in effect how she can lift herself up by her own bootstraps. "Where do I go from here?" (66) But the circumstances may well be such that there is *no* exit, within her present terms of reference.

Sometimes, however, Mrs. Jackson does not express despair but only uncertainty. "I feel better every day—at least, I think so. But I don't know what's going to happen" (56). She does not know for sure whether she will be *able* to go back to work when her six months' sick leave are up, or even (between you and me) whether they will want her.

More or less at the same time, though, especially in 73–77 and 101–107, she expresses an attitude that is almost at the opposite pole, a mood somewhere within that nexus made up of optimism, hope, confidence, and the like. Part of the present task is to be sufficiently precise in delineating the features of this aspect of her feelings to understand them, both in themselves, and in relation to the seemingly opposite feelings of hopelessness, despair, or whatever it is.

One feature that has already suggested caution in labelling her happier moods "hope," has been the observation that the slightest physical and situational changes influence her disproportionately. Her attitudes fluctuate constantly, not with wild changes of effect, but in her relatively calm (dangerously so?) intellectual appraisal of her future.

Elements are present in her statements that perhaps reflect a concomitant of the "pride" previously discussed. She cannot really believe that the "temporary" replacement could possibly be doing as good a job as she did, let alone a better one (64). And the grandiosity of expecting to produce an oil painting of a caliber to "show" in a matter of days, and considering this hobby as a potential means of supporting the family almost passes belief (64 and 105).

Another aspect of the puzzle is the relation to "reality" of either of these poles in her mood swings. This issue seems to be acute particularly when she sounds more hopeful—in the light of external appraisals of both her physical prognosis and her occupational future, not to mention the improbability that latent genius is about to be manifested on canvas to a dazzled world. Where she speaks of the future "bringing" things (101 f.), she, strictly speaking, means *better* things. She is not being stoical, let alone Christian. And it is what appears to me to be the unrealism of this implied optimism that irritates me to the point of arguing with her. I respond as if I want to shake a little sense into her: "My good woman, can't you grasp that . . . !" One does not deny that this is how she consciously sees and feels things, but the question of objective reality obtrudes. And if her hopes are in fact an illusion, what does this imply with respect to her opposite mood? Does it mean that she has not truly experienced despair yet either? Or is it more likely that the despair is "real" and overwhelming, and the "hopes" just a cover-up?

In any case, notably lacking in Mrs. Jackson's ups and downs is a basic trust in God, whatever comes. There is little evidence of a realistic acceptance of the unyielding limits of the givenness of some things, let alone confidence that God is working alongside of one within them even though they may be unalterable. (This way of stating it correctly implies that my own Christian experience matches the Revised Standard Version of Rom. 8:28 as over against the King James Version, whatever the purely textual considerations. "We know that in everything God works for good with those who love him, . . ." rather than "All things work together for good to them that love God. . . .") This is why her pat response of: "Oh, well. We'll just have to wait and see what the future brings" (101) seems so farcical—because if it does not bring the quite specific better things she wants for her family and herself, she won't tolerate it!

One further related point is the terribly difficult problem for a person in revising his expectations and satisfactions downward. This is part and parcel of retirement for the individual, as it is on a national scale for Britain in having to adjust to being a second-class power. Mr. Jackson has had to face it prematurely. And Mrs. Jackson is resisting it with all her might. (It would seem probable that suicides might frequently occur in this context, or at least that this problem would be important in status-integration theories of suicide.) Yet without wishing to be trite or simple-mindedly pious, it seems to me that real Christian hope becomes a greater possibility in all this, as her "false" hopes collapse one by one. Precisely when there is nothing left but total despair in human and temporal terms, and perhaps only then, it may become possible to shift the focus and basis of her hopes to the Eternal.

A quite different line of reflection also suggests itself on the basis of this *alternation* of her attitude (her fluctuations of mood induced by quite minor changes in circumstances have already been mentioned). Important to note in passing is the warning implicit here with regard to the value of a single visit or verbatim. For if too limited a biopsy, as it were, had been taken, the swings, themselves a telltale sign of trouble, might well have been missed. One might have met Mrs. Jackson when she was "high" and hopeful, or when she was "blue" and despairing. And then, for all the limitations noted with respect to either of these moods by itself, the fuller picture revealed precisely by the temporal oscillations would have been missed.

But the problem goes much deeper than this. For there is an element of changeability that is intrinsic to creatureliness. We are *not* consistent, dependable, steadfast people with respect to moods, attitudes, opinions, and intentions. The resolves and feelings of even the most mature and saintly of men must surely waver at times. (Granted, Mrs. Jackson's swings of outlook appear to be rather extreme, if not in their intensity at least with respect to the tenuous stimuli that occasion them.) This would seem to call for a careful analysis of such valued characteristics as steadfastness, reliability, and fidelity. To what extent are these even possible? What does faithfulness "on and off" mean, and look like?

It should be noted that this is a different, though related, issue from the one raised under "Pastoral Theology" in Chapter II. There it was the significance of the sequence of developmental *stages* that was in question. Here it is the apparent tension between some of the qualities of maturity themselves. It is more than a problem of the relation of human hopes to "reality." Man's vital capacity for responsiveness seemingly includes an innate susceptibility to changes of mood and outlook. And the latter tend to militate against qualities such as stability, which imply firmness and durability.

# III

## MR. JACKSON—MAY

### INTRODUCTION

I had had several previous contacts with Mr. Jackson. In February of last year I met him for the first time when he was admitted to the hospital for total exhaustion, following the loss of his job a couple of days before. He was being philosophical about it, talking in terms of it being the best thing in the long run and expecting to find something else easily enough. Five months later he was hospitalized again, this time for loss of balance and falling. He had not been working for the past five months. This was an amiable but fairly shallow visit, and again he was discharged before my next call at the hospital.

In March of this year, I had four visits with him during a ten-day period in hospital for anxiety. He was very shaky and troubled, but toward the end of this period was able to unload freely and intimately. His doctor was trying a new kind of hypno-talk treatment with him. He still had not had any work until quite recently, when he had found a different kind of job which had no prospects and was a great strain on him.

On the present occasion he was admitted to the hospital with drug intoxication of his whole system. The first short visit found him still very stuporous. Two days later, according to my notes, he was feeling better and brighter: things are on the mend now—having really "hit the bottom," they're on the way up. Don't know how far they'll go, but at least they're going up. He is greatly impressed with the improvement of his wife, which he sees as being a result of her having had electroshock treatments, of which he highly approves. She is "not so antagonistic and bitter toward everyone, including me. She had good cause to be, but she's not any more." He thinks he'll get a job in the big city. His recent job, although completely out of his line, had given him some confidence—despite the fact that the irregular hours, combined with tranquilizers on an empty stomach, had led to his hospitalization. He thinks his drafting experience ought to be valuable to somebody. He would waive pension rights and start on a low salary if the prospects were good. His brother is now fully cognizant of the situation, and Mr. Jackson said he is willing to take his advice, perhaps to the extent of changing houses and dropping his private golf club membership, etc. However, despite some verbalizing of the necessity for lowering his standard of living and his expectations, he didn't really convince me of his concrete gut-level acceptance of this or of his determination to start taking the necessary steps. He still sounded too confident that the problem could be licked.

The two visits that followed this took place jointly with his wife, and have already been noted in Chapter II. They were remarkable chiefly for the way in which husband and wife talked their own line almost as if the other was not there. When I talked to him next, five days later, it was in the presence of a young man in the next bed, who joined in the first part of the visit. We continued along the lines on which they had been talking when I arrived. Again, the details were recorded in note form only.

Mr. Jackson sees the main issue, for the doctors and for him, as being whether or not he can live without drugs, on which he has relied for years. (At one point he said, in agreement with what I had understood from Mrs. Jackson, that he had been relying on drugs "for ten years.") He freely acknowledges that reliance on drugs is not any normative ideal for "health." But he wonders whether his "normal," i.e., without-drugs, state is one of such panic that he will *have* to have some drugs in order to function at all—much as a diabetic has to be stabilized at some level. His doctor is apparently going to have some more specialists examine him—because last week he told Mr. Jackson that he was now completely off drugs, and that night he had a *grand mal* seizure. Doctor Singh admitted that the specialists would probably all come up with different answers. And Mr. Jackson has no confidence in such "experts" at all, believing that they tend to generalize on the basis of the success or failure they have had with a very few vaguely similar cases.

During this visit, there was a telephone call concerning an outstanding debt. Mr. Jackson explained to the caller his present physical state, and also that his brother was looking after his financial affairs. He was quite open and apparently casual about this to his roommate and me afterward, perhaps aided by being sedated, and he admired the persistence of the creditor's agent for having tracked him down to the hospital.

Mr. Jackson is not hard to visit, inasmuch as he talks freely but also rather slowly. I had never written up my conversations with him, and perhaps by and large this did not matter too much, but I particularly regret not having a record of two of the conversations from his stay in the hospital during March, two months prior to this.

The following forty-minute conversation with Mr. Jackson, alone after the first few minutes, occurred on the following day.

## CONVERSATION

*Relative:*   109   (*To me as I entered the room and she was about to leave*) You're going to have a lot of listening to do!

*Mr. J.:*   110   (*To relative—and they continued for three or four minutes*) But I don't like it—a furnished room on Bank Street!

*Relative:*   111   No, I didn't think you would. But it may be the best for all concerned.

*Mr. J.:*   112   It won't be the best for me. Don't I get any say at all? I know I can't decide anything lying here, flat on my back. But at least I would think I ought to be in on the committee that decides, and hear what goes on, and get a vote.

*Relative:*   113   Well, it's still a long way from a decision yet. I'm neither for it or against it.

*Mr. J.:*   114   But I'm against it! Don't I get a say?

*Relative:*   115   Yes, you get a say, of course.

*Mr. J.:*   116   Well, put me down for one vote against being put in a one-room flat on Bank Street— strongly against.

*Relative:*   117   That sounds like the title of a book.

*Mr. J.:*   118   It is, more or less.

*Relative:*   119   (*To me*) We're working from the youngest up. We've got David and Barbara settled, thanks to Father Dawson. And an aunt is taking Lily this weekend, to live with her in Birmingham. Do you know she only went to school a day and a half last week? She sat around the house and watched television. On Wednesday she went to the cinema, and she spent the day in the city on Friday. That's no

good. But she'll be able to go to a grammar
school in Birmingham, starting next week. (*To
me*) Well, you've got a lot of listening to do.
Cheerio, Jack.

Mr. J.: 120 I'll say you have. I don't like it at all. They're
splitting my family up, just like that, without
so much as a "by your leave." Oh, I agree
that David and Barbara need to be out of the
situation as it is now, and to live in a home.
And it'll be good for Lily. This way she can
take her "A" levels in the summer, and go on
to the university—which she wouldn't have
been ready for if she stuck around here.

But they didn't consult me—they didn't
even tell me! And after all, I am their father.
It just came out when Janet popped in to see
me. She was talking, and said something,
"Well, at least we won't have to bother about
Lily for the rest of the year." And I said,
"What do you mean?" And she said, "You
know what's happening, don't you?" And I
said, "No, I don't. Tell me." And she told me
that they had sent her up to my older sister's.

Minister: 121 So while you approve of the solutions they've
arrived at, you don't like the way they were
made at all.

Mr. J.: 122 No, I don't. After all, I'm their father. And a
man wants to bring up his own family, and
have them around him. It's put the Mrs. right
back—to worse than she was before she came
into the hospital. They're just not paying any
attention to the main problem, which is just
to get me back on my feet and working. And
splitting up the family just makes me feel
worse.

| | | |
|---|---|---|
| *Minister:* | 123 | It makes you feel depressed, that they are taking it all completely out of your hands. |
| *Mr. J.:* | 124 | Not depressed, no. |
| *Minister:* | 125 | Angry? |
| *Mr. J.:* | 126 | No. (*Would he dare be angry, with the risk of alienating them entirely?*) Hurt, deeply hurt. I've always been a fairly sensitive person. And to do this all behind my back, and not even to tell me about it—that hurts. And we can manage. Janet is a fairly responsible member of the community now. She has a job. And all I need is to get emotionally pulled together and get a job. And this knocks me back. A furnished room on Bank Street! And the family split up all over the place! |
| *Minister:* | 127 | You don't at all see this as a way of getting stabilized and on your feet, and then drawing your family together again? (*Here I reflect that he emphatically did not.*) |
| *Mr. J.:* | 128 | No, I don't. At least they might let me have one member of the family living with me. Otherwise, why should I bother? What's the point? |
| *Minister:* | 129 | It would be a meaningless existence, because it would be apart from everything that has meaning for you. |
| *Mr. J.:* | 130 | Damn right it would! After all, that's not too much to ask, is it, that a man be allowed to look after his own family? And I did it for eighteen years. I had a good job with Mather's. And the wife worked if and when she wanted to, and any money she earned was— was an extra. |
| *Minister:* | 131 | For luxuries? |
| *Mr. J.:* | 132 | Yes. It's only this past year I've been out of |

a job. But they treat me as if I couldn't look after the family. It's Nan Lloyd's idea. She was talking to me on the telephone this morning, and came up with it. Her first husband was an alcoholic, like me, and relied a lot on drugs. And they got him to go off and live by himself and he did quite well. And therefore she thinks it's the solution for me—but I'm not the same person as him. They all act as if I was a hophead, which I'm not. It's grossly unfair. But I'm not in a position to challenge them.

*Minister:*    133    Even though you don't like it, at the moment you have to rely on them to a considerable extent.

*Mr. J.:*    134    Yeah. But it's the way they do it. There's a few old bills, and so on. Well, I can't take care of them at the moment. But they'll all get paid. And my brother is looking after that. He's a banker, with guineas in his veins instead of blood, warm blood. And he won't lose by it. The house will have to be sold. But once I get a job, it'll be all right.

And the sister-in-law is sharp. She hurts me a lot, just the way she will say things. She doesn't know it, but she hurts. She acts as if I was a waster. In fact she said, if I had been a success this would never have happened. And they treat me as if I were a nuisance. In fact she makes it clear that I am, rather than acting in a spirit of Christian charity.

*Minister:*    135    Which makes you feel completely worthless, and a trouble to everybody.

*Mr. J.:*    136    It sure does. And when I'm trying to get back my emotional and psychological stability, whatever the difference is, it doesn't help at

all. In fact, it makes me very depressed indeed. But they all seem to have worked it
out together: my brother and sister-in-law,
the Lloyds, and Dr. Singh. They've simply
decided what they're going to do with us.
And it has made Mrs. Jackson worse, I know
it has. In fact, she can't take it any longer,
and is going away to stay with a friend. Oh,
yes, she told my brother to make whatever
decisions seemed best to him, and so did I.
But they don't help by the way they go about
it. God, it makes me depressed! [*cf. 124!*]

Minister:    137    Instead of treating you like a human being
with concern for you as a person and a family,
they are treating it like a problem situation
to be solved in the most economical and ef-
ficient way.

Mr. J.:      138    Yes, they don't treat me as a person at all. I
don't know what the future holds. Dr. Singh
was in for three minutes this morning, and I
don't know whether I'll see anyone else today. You, of course, and you count. But I'm
not going to get any better just lying here.
I don't know when I've ever felt so depressed
in all my life. It looks completely hopeless.

Minister:    139    Hopeless for you personally or the family as
a whole?

Mr. J.:      140    Yes, me personally. And now the family is
getting spread apart. And the wife is worse
—and what if she should want her job back?
And what with the way they treat me! My
sister-in-law has never had sympathy or personal concern. It's not as if they were helping
me in a Christian way. I'm regarded as a
nuisance, and if you asked them they would
tell you, "Yes, he's a nuisance."

*Minister:*   141   Which doesn't help one little bit to make you feel that you are significant or worthwhile.

*Mr. J.:*   142   But they don't dig that! They've no understanding of the person. If I was in their shoes, or if I was trying to help someone in my situation, I'd listen to them, and try and understand them and how they felt.

*Minister:*   143   Well, Mr. Jackson, you can be assured of this: there is nothing I can do to solve the "problem situation," but I will continue to listen to you as a person, and be concerned about how you feel.

*Mr. J.:*   144   I know you will, and that's important. I value the opportunity to tell someone how depressing and hopeless it all seems. And it helps me to get back a little on an even keel for a while.

*Minister:*   145   Well, I am going to have to go now. (*The cleaners and a nurse had been waiting for some time, and I had a meeting.*) But I want to assure you that you matter as a person to me, and more than that, that you are important to God.

*Mr. J.:*   146   Thank you very much. If only the others acted the same way. (*He showed signs of reverting to the situation.*)

*Minister:*   147   Well, I will be back either tomorrow or Friday.

*Mr. J.:*   148   Please do come when you can.

## Further Conversation

This visit took place two days later. I had called on Mr. Jackson earlier in the morning. He had obviously been asleep, and, once I promised to come back later, admitted that he would prefer that. As I returned a few minutes before the time we had agreed on, I found him checking on the time with one of the nurses. Throughout this thirty-five-minute visit, he lay full-length on the bed with just his head raised and against the headboard, with no movement and almost no facial expression or vocal inflection after he settled down.

*Mr. J.:*  149  I've just been talking with the Mrs. on the phone, and she chewed me out.

*Minister:*  150  Oh?

*Mr. J.:*  151  Yes—about the cottage in the Lake District that we have, you know. She's quite adamant about not selling it. She was on about how she had worked for ten years for that cottage, and scrubbed floors for ten years before that, and that she absolutely refuses to let it be sold. She ignores the fact that I've worked a hell of a lot longer than that for this family —and contributed the money that I inherited.

She's quite unreasonable about the house here, too. She isn't going to have anything to do with buying a new one. She's just leaving it to me. And I don't think that's something a chap can do alone, just buy a house, and hope that his wife is going to like it. That's not doing things as a partnership. And as I see it, marriage should be a partnership. And she doesn't realize that it's one thing to talk about selling our house, and quite another thing to do it. From my experience, I know that you put a house up for sale with the estate agents, but you don't expect to sell it the next day. It might still be there a year from now. In fact, my estate agent tells me that our kind of house is a particularly difficult one to sell.

*Minister:*  152   You feel that all the responsibility and the decisions are being dumped on you, without any help, and they're not easy to make.

*Mr. J.:*  153   That's right. And then there's this business of the "committee" deciding that I should live alone. And that's no good—that won't help me. It's not a question of maturity or immaturity. I've done it before, as a bachelor, and also shared a flat with other chaps. But a man needs to have someone to live with. That's why I want Janet to stay with me, for two reasons. Firstly, she has the Morris at the moment—she needs it to get to work. But I don't want to be stuck without a car. And if she stayed with me we would both get to use it. And the second thing is for company. Of course, I wouldn't expect her to be around all the time. She would be out a lot—but at least there would be someone around some of the time. It wouldn't have to be Janet. It could be one of the others. But there's the two reasons for Janet. She's got the car, and this way we would both get to use it. And we're close. We've got along well together lately. In fact, I think that Janet and I are closer now than the Mrs. and I. She's so tense all the time, and always getting onto the children. And she chewed me and the children out over the phone. She says she can't forget their lying and cheating and forging, and seems to hold it against all of them, and against me. And I don't think that's any good, and it doesn't help me at all. I can't operate like this.

*Minister:*  154   You feel that, even if it's not being used against you at the moment, that the past is being stored up, ready to be used.

Mr. J.:  155  Yeah. And when you're making a fresh start these things have to be forgotten. I've forgotten them. But she gets onto the children for everything, and that gets me upset. She's always, I suspect, had what I call a "low motherhood quotient." Oh, she likes the kids. At least, I suppose she does. But she has never shown them a lot of affection and so on.

At this point we were interrupted by a nurse searching for a previous patient's garment, which led Mr. Jackson to remember that his own dressing gown had disappeared; and by a volunteer checking name tabs and beds. Then his doctor arrived. I had been present and welcome while Dr. Singh had visited before, and throughout the following conversation, after preliminary bows for the tributes doctor and patient paid me to one another, sat back and listened to this fascinating dialogue. Dr. Singh throughout was brisk and straight down the middle (i.e., pitching right over the plate).

Doctor:  156  How are you feeling today?

Mr. J.:  157  Not bad, considering everything, but—

Doctor:  158  Well, I just stopped in to put you in the picture on a couple of things. The first is that we hope to have you out of this bed soon. We are going to reduce the drugs slowly, according to a systematic schedule.

Mr. J.:  159  They've already been cut down.

Doctor:  160  Not the little white ones. We're going to cut that out in the middle of the day. The whole thing will be carefully controlled, with constant checks. But we want you to be able to stand up on your own without them.

And the second thing is that the subcommittee is meeting on Sunday. And we'll either come in and talk to you about what we have decided, or one of us will if the rest can't manage.

Mr. J.:     161   So I don't get to sit on the subcommittee?

Doctor:     162   Sunday afternoon is the only time we could all manage. I have a meeting tonight that I must go to. And we thought of Saturday afternoon, but John has something on then. We agree that you must be kept fully informed about the proceedings. But John pointed out that it's not easy to talk about a person in his presence—at least in the early stages. So I'll be in to let you know what happened. (*Moving away.*)

Mr. J.:     163   Now, don't rush off straightaway. There's some things you ought to know, to put before the subcommittee when it meets. The wife rang up this morning—I've already told the minister most of this—threatening to commit suicide if we sold the cottage. She was quite definite about it.

Doctor:     164   Well, now let's get things straight. It would be nice not to have to sell it. I know how she feels. We had a somewhat similar situation when the war started. We had a little place in the Cotswolds, but we just had to let it go. It's a matter of priorities.

Mr. J.:     165   The rates are very low.

Doctor:     166   I should hope they are, in the Lake District. But of what use is the house to you, in your present situation?

Mr. J.:     167   And she also refuses to have anything to do with getting rid of the house in town. She wants me to do it all.

| *Doctor:* | 168 | It's in both your names, isn't it? So you'll have to get her signature. But there's a lot of unrealism going on here, that we'll have to break through. I remember my father once saying, when I was engaged and so were the people in both the neighboring houses: "We're knee-deep in love here." Well, we're about ankle-deep in unrealism. We can get out of it—but it can't just be left as it is. |
|---|---|---|
| *Mr. J.:* | 169 | Yes. But we've also got to recognize that selling this house may not be so easy. You don't just put it up for sale one day and get rid of it the next. In fact, I know from my own experience in the business (?) that this kind of house is particularly difficult to sell. It may take a year. And Mrs. Jackson is not going to help in buying a new one. She wants me to make all the decisions myself, about its size, layout, and so on. |
| *Doctor:* | 170 | Well, there'll be plenty of time to think about that later. For the meantime, you'll not be needing one. |
| *Mr. J.:* | 171 | I want to live in a home, not a one-room flat. And I know what size we shall need. |
| *Doctor:* | 172 | Well, for the moment that is not important. Where you live, that is home—wherever you hang your hat is home. And perhaps you will talk to your wife on the phone and try and help her understand about the cottage. |
| *Mr. J.:* | 173 | No, I can't do that. She has made it quite clear that she regards herself as having worked all her life for that cottage, and that if it is sold she will commit suicide. And I think that should be reckoned in the cost! |
| *Doctor:* | 174 | Of course that should be reckoned in the cost, and I'm glad you let me know. I'll have to |

talk with her psychiatrist about this, because this is one of the aspects of reality that he should be helping her face. I was just suggesting that we ought to establish an order of priority in the financial obligations.

Mr. J.: 175 What order of priority?

Doctor: 176 No, I don't mean a particular list. But to say that an order of financial obligations has to be established. And then if she raises the matter of the cottage, we can talk about it. But I agree with you that the house here is much more important first of all. Let me see your hands: hold them out. (*Routine check.*)

Mr. J.: 177 Look, that's pretty steady. (*And it was.*)

Doctor: 178 Very good. Remember that if you feel you need it, I can get you a little help [i.e., alcohol]. Especially in the morning, when things are worst, I can order a little if you feel you need it.

Mr. J.: 179 I reckon I'm all right at the moment, I can do without it. But I thought the committee ought to know about the phone call.

Doctor: 180 They ought indeed, and I'm very grateful to you for making me aware of it, and I'll see they all get to know. Well, keep smiling. I'll be in again. (*To me*) Good-by, sir.

I stayed long enough after this for Mr. Jackson to comment and express his feelings, which amazingly showed no overt hostility at the treatment he was getting. Mainly, conventionally, he expressed again his concern that his wife's reaction was part of the cost that had to be taken into account, and that her life could not just be ignored. The whole incident was reminiscent of an international conference table, with the weaker nation getting some minor concessions in return for going along with the basic decisions of the major powers. But the rabid insistence on independence, even by the small nation virtually subsisting on foreign aid, was notably missing. A voice at the conference table this man wants. But he is never going to sever his connections by a walkout, or so it seemed.

## Pastoral Care

Seeing the other side of the picture is enough to banish any easy optimism about finding "the best solution for all concerned." The family circumstances have reached a point where some decisions *have* to be made and some practical steps taken. The solution toward which the "committee of five" inclines in the light of the total situation includes the element of splitting up the family that had suggested itself to me independently. But even if it is the best that can be done, it will be important not to ignore the individual suffering that this will entail. And the pain of being split up as a family will be intensified for the adults by the necessity of reducing their standard of living—a hard enough task even when other conditions are optimal.

These two conversations between Mr. Jackson and the minister lend themselves particularly well to being discussed within the framework of Carl Rogers' theories. For whatever the detailed limitation of the minister's responses as an embodiment of client-centered attitudes, in contrast to the approach of the relative and the doctor they seem almost a paradigm. And Mr. Jackson talked of his feelings a great deal, though without marked effect, perhaps as a consequence of medication.

As the minister entered the scene, Mr. Jackson was expressing himself to a relative with regard to the decisions that had already been made by the "committee of five" who were helping to straighten out the family situation. Overtly, it is not the decisions themselves that Mr. Jackson objects to, but the manner in which they were made. Even though it was a matter of splitting the family up hither and yon, he was not even consulted. This makes him feel extremely hurt, rather than angry or depressed (123–126)—although a little later he mentions not knowing when he has felt so depressed in his whole life (136–138). He gets the clear impression that he is regarded as a nuisance (134, 140), a waster, a failure as a father-provider (132–134), and an addict to boot! The external situation is bad enough. And this must be a further crushing blow to his self-respect, which can be no more than knee-high to a grasshopper anyway, although he doesn't admit it. Thus whether, "torn from the bosom of his family" (as he sees it), he will have the motivation to work and provide for them again remains doubtful. And of course, this "solution" is a ready excuse to fall back on in the event of subsequent failure.

As Mr. Jackson himself sees it, the first priority is to get him back on his feet and working again (122), to get emotionally pulled together and find a job (126). He stresses that he did function as a father-provider for eighteen years (130). And he looks forward to a fresh start. But he passes over his inability to find or persevere in a job over the past year or two, and his several collapses, in complete silence. With respect to the sale of their town house, he is unwilling to take the initiative and responsibility, basing his plea here on a "partnership" concept of marriage. In his reiterated dislike of the proposed solution, he did not give any detailed consideration to concrete alternatives. Nor did he openly recognize that the family situation has reached rock bottom, although he is surprisingly frank in admitting to specific crises such as his debts.

In short, there is a considerable discrepancy between the way Mr. Jackson thinks of himself, the person he perceives himself as being, and the self he experiences in the way others regard him and treat him. By and large, he overtly rejects or denies his experience and clings to his idealized self-concept. Reality is all around him, pressing in on him to his discomfort.

But he does not appear ready to work at the discrepancy between his perceived self and his experience. The other helpers have not been concerned to facilitate this, of course. They have stepped into a crisis situation to bring some order out of chaos for all six members of the family. Nor is this to be negative about their efforts. For all that we know, this may have been literally the last straw. But they *are* seemingly more concerned with getting a job done than with Mr. Jackson's sensitivities and whether he likes it or not.

In contrast, the minister listens to Mr. Jackson in the attempt to understand how he sees the situation and feels about it. Theoretically, it should be therapeutic for Mr. Jackson to be treated with warm respect and have attentive concern shown for his feelings, besides not feeling that things are being imposed on him or that he is being judged and found wanting. In the security and warmth of such a relationship, the individual should become freer to really express and explore his feelings, experiences, and self-perceptions. But Rogers goes on to point out that "this clearer perception is in itself disrupting and anxiety-creating, not therapeutic." [13] But when these new, disturbing feelings are also reflected, with continuing regard and without evaluation, the individual is enabled to begin to work through his difficulties. The incongruity between self-concept and experience can be diminished. And in becoming more congruent, according to Rogers' theory, he will be more open to his experience, more able to evaluate his experience, more realistic, and will also have more positive regard for himself. Thus he will better be able to estimate his reality and his possibilities, and to make more effective decisions accordingly.

The goal of client-centered therapy has been variously expressed as a "fully-functioning person," a person "being one's self," and "a mature person." But before we examine these in relation to Mr. Jackson, some comments must be made about the whole family context. For the problem situation has reached a state where it *has* to be dealt with in some way.

There is no question of there being time to help Mr. Jackson to achieve these eminently desirable goals so that he is able personally to work on the total crisis. Thus the very possibility of my relating to him as I did was made enormously easier by, if not absolutely predicated on, the fact that a group of concerned people were taking on the responsibility for sorting out the problem situation. If this had not been happening already, it would have been incumbent on me to help along these lines, and a purely reflective approach would have been ruled out.

Even with this freedom to be client-centered with Mr. Jackson, there remain several serious questions about its effectiveness. First, there is a slight suspicion as to the source of the feelings that Mr. Jackson claims. At first sight, I am tempted to pat myself on the back when the feeling of being "depressed," which he pushed aside at 124, is espoused in 134 and 136. I gauged his feelings more accurately than he did himself! Then, too, it is warming to be told that he feels I treated him like a person—while he feels his relatives do not so regard him (144). But in both these instances, it may well have been little more than an echo, for the root expression originally came from me. He may simply have been playing back what he thought I wanted to hear from slight cues he picked up.

Mr. Jackson appears to lap up the reflection of his feelings. Since his relatives have tended to communicate with him only to present a brief report of executive decisions already made, such treatment is like water to a thirsty man. But there remains another niggling doubt: is it really good for him? It might just possibly reinforce his defenses, convincing him that his self-concept is accurate and that these other clods are simply unable to perceive his competence. It is evident that Mr. Jackson did not even start to work on his problem in the way Rogers predicts, though he supposedly perceived the relationship with the minister to be facilitating. But this may simply have been a function of the brevity and truncated nature of the relationship. This raises a significant theoretical issue, even for those who grant the desirability of this approach in

sustained counseling and where there is the ability to imple-
ment it. What is the effectiveness, if any, of a partial dose of
client-centered therapy?

Finally, the issue of a multitude of helpers employing diverse approaches again raises its head. Moreover, it presents
something of an extreme case for a commonly discussed theoretical issue. It has frequently been asked in terms of the power
of the therapeutic relationship and experience to generalize
itself thereafter. A man receives positive regard, acceptance,
and empathetic reflection from the counselor—but then has
to return to a social context where these experiences are unlikely to receive much reinforcement. With respect to Mr.
Jackson, it is probable that they will be directly and unani-
mously contradicted in favor of the proposition that he is a
worthless failure. The power that has to be generated by the
experience with the counselor in order for it, not merely to be
generalized, but to compensate for widespread ongoing contrary experiences would seem to be enormous.

## PASTORAL THEOLOGY

Again, there are doubtless many worthwhile directions in
which theological reflection on the material of this chapter
could be pursued, not least with respect to the pastoral approach adopted and its potential witness to God caring for
Mr. Jackson as he is. However, that is a subject which has
been written about at length, albeit not from the same starting
point.[14] In the present section the focus of the theologizing
will be restricted to the phenomenon of dependence and its
ramifications, which is so sharply raised by the case material.

Even from the available conversations, many indicators of
Mr. Jackson's dependent life-style over the years can readily
be discovered. Several remarks are suggestive of a history of
some degree of reliance on alcohol, for one thing. Mrs. Jackson
implies this by her comments (56, 62). The fact that the doc-

tor volunteered to prescribe "a little help" if things were bad in the mornings points in the same direction (178). And if further proof is needed, Mr. Jackson refers to himself as an alcoholic (132), though without elaborating on what he means by this.

The evidence of long-term and heavy dependence on drugs is still stronger. Mrs. Jackson mentions that his reliance on tranquilizers began ten years before (60), and caustically observes that "he's got to learn that he can't depend on pills to solve all his problems" (62). Drug intoxication is the reason for his present hospitalization, of course, and the doctor is working on the reduction of this immediate crisis and the long-term management of his condition (158–160). While Mr. Jackson strenuously objects to being regarded as a "hophead" by his relatives, his own perception of the issue, as reported in the introduction to this chapter, is whether or not he *can* live and function without the aid of drugs.

Alcohol and drugs, then, have been two overt physiological crutches. But along with this, there are other comments that suggest either personal inadequacy or undue reliance on other people of a long-standing nature. According to Mrs. Jackson, they both thought it best that he should take the job with the least strain involved after the end of the Second World War (99). And at one point his not changing jobs—with unforeseeable but unfortunate consequences—is thought by Mrs. Jackson to have been a result of her dissuading him (101). Latterly, he has been unable to find satisfactory employment over nearly two years, even granting the probability that originally he set his sights far too high. And now, in the hospital, there is his unwillingness to go ahead and take the necessary steps to sell their home without his wife's active participation, whatever that signifies.

Overall, as Chapter I proposed, there is little doubt that Mrs. Jackson has been the dominant member in the family. It is very possible that this met some of Mr. Jackson's needs as well as some of hers. Nevertheless, it is also the case that given this support he was apparently able to function reasonably adequately (albeit, not without drink or pills) for many years, so long as he had a stable occupation that he could both cope with and respect. With sudden unemployment, followed by the total collapse of the family situation, however, Mr. Jackson's disintegration begins to appear rather severe.

Admittedly having little power to do anything about it, he has allowed a committee of friends, relatives, and doctor to take over the management of his family's affairs. He dislikes the decisions made, and the manner of their making still more. Yet he is not ready to antagonize the committee to the point where they abandon the responsibility they have assumed. (He does not even express very much anger toward them to me, a neutral third party, where it would be safe.) He needs them, and gives the impression of being quite acceptant of this dependency. And he also states fairly emphatically that he needs his family for life to be worthwhile, and wants at least one of them to live with him under the new regime.

Theologically, the situation here appears at first sight to be almost the obverse of that considered in Chapter I. There, the difficulty for "the strong one," the managing, controlling individual, facing up to her creatureliness and dependence on God was apparent. A distorted autonomy, a false independence, appeared to aggravate the problem of entering into a right relationship with God in Mrs. Jackson's case. So it might be expected that this would be simplified for a man seemingly devoid of "pride." But turning to Mr. Jackson, the "dependent" one in the family constellation, it appears a little, if any, less difficult for him to depend appropriately on God. Probably not very convincing to Mr. Jackson would be the exhortation in I Peter 5:7, "You can throw the whole weight of your anxieties upon him, for you are his personal concern" (J. B. Phillips, *The New Testament in Modern English*; The Macmillan Company, 1958). For God does not seem likely to cushion

his falls, protect him, and hold his hand as he craves. Moreover, God will probably not "take over" and simply issue clear-
cut instructions as to what has to be done next, as the
committee of five is willing to do.

Presumably, then, Mr. Jackson demonstrates a distorted
dependence that is quite different from the trusting commitment of a mature self into God's keeping. Fitting this into a
taxonomy of sinfulness is not the most important task. But we
have noted that in some ways it is the mirror image of Mrs.
Jackson's "pride" and distorted self-dependence. And since
we shall be turning to Reinhold Niebuhr's analysis of "pride"
in Chapter V, it is worth querying whether Mr. Jackson's life
fits into Niebuhr's other basic category of sin, "sensuality."

This leads to the more important question of the extent to
which Mr. Jackson's life-style is willful, a chosen "easy way
out" of coping with life and its myriad possibilities and problems. Is it a form of the failure to be a self, of which Goldstein
has written, although for different and more reprehensible
reasons? [15] Or does it mainly reflect a coming to terms with
basic, constitutional inadequacy, severe limitation to the self
that he has the power to become? These are some of the questions my talks with Mr. Jackson raise for me theologically.
The point of them is not to assess his accountability for what
he has become. That is God's business. But to understand why
Mr. Jackson became the way he is is necessary in order to answer the question, "Where do we go from here?"

It is one thing to advocate "commitment" to the adolescent
—who is becoming well aware that his parents are fallible and
is already in the process of loosening the apron strings that
have bound him to them—in terms of reposing his ultimate
trust in God. But in Mr. Jackson's case we are confronted by
a way of life, not just an appropriate developmental task.
Moreover, his reliance on others does not appear to be identical with trusting them. When any particular source of support fails, he immediately casts around for another one, and

appears to be satisfied with that so long as it functions.

It seems to me that the general theoretical issue underlying the various aspects of this problem is that of the nature and extent of the continuities and/or discontinuities between dependence on human others and dependence on God. Are these identical processes in terms of their dynamics, merely distinguished by a shift to a more ultimate object-person at an appropriate developmental stage? Or can mature dependence on God, like the creative interdependence of two persons being-themselves-together in marriage, only follow on the establishment of a measure of genuine identity and autonomy? Or should the discriminating criterion between what is healthy and what is not be the balance between dependence and independence in relation to the age and capacities of the person concerned?

In the present catastrophic situation, when the former crutches have all failed or turned on him, the fact of Mr. Jackson's incapacity and helplessness is starkly evident—perhaps the more so because "outsiders" have temporarily stepped in and taken over management of the family situation. The theological, and also very practical question for ministry is: How can Mr. Jackson's escape from his bondage best be facilitated? Thornton's basic thesis is that the optimal penultimate approach is the one that fosters and favors "health." [16] But supposing we grant this, what is indicated in the present case? It is clear that it would not be desirable for Mr. Jackson simply to substitute one compulsive dependence (on God) for another (on other people), as the alcoholic sometimes uses Alcoholics Anonymous in a way identical to the function originally served by the contents of the bottle. But what ought to be done, and how to do it, are considerably harder to see. Is it necessary to help Mr. Jackson to stand on his own feet, so that God can speak with him? How can he be helped to see that ultimately he cannot rely on others with any more success than on himself, so that he can move toward trust in God?

# IV

## PASTORAL CARE

In this chapter, attention is turned to several areas of concern for the ministry of pastoral care. Admittedly, many aspects of the problems here discussed have been raised for me at other points in my ministry, teaching, and thinking. The subjects seem to fit better in a separate chapter not only because they merit more general discussion than would have been appropriate within the context of specific reflection on the relationship with the Jacksons, but also because consideration of the issues will not be limited to whatever light is shed upon them by the case material. On the other hand, I have tried to be disciplined in restricting attention to problems some aspect of which at least does arise in the context of the ministry to the Jacksons, and to refrain from taking up any number of other "bees in my pastoral bonnet." From among the numerous problems worthy of sustained attention that are raised by the case, the selection of the four areas that are treated was determined by personal interest.

## THE SINGLE CASE

What value has a single case? What does it prove? This is an important methodological question, and one that has logical priority, for the significance of the discussion of substantive issues that follows partly hinges on the answer given at this point.

In the modern world, the categories in which we think, the data we consider impressive, even the kinds of questions we ask, have all been pervasively influenced by the natural sciences and the social sciences. Politicians, manufacturers, salesmen, and television sponsors are all absorbingly interested in the quest for regularities, the normal distributions of the potential electorate, market, or viewing public, what "the average person" thinks, wants, and needs—or can be persuaded that he does. This emphasis is part of the atmosphere in which we live, and to avoid absorbing it is as difficult as to avoid breathing the very air around us. So, we are always in danger of being beguiled by the criteria of those fields in which successful prediction is supposed to be the acid test of skill, truth, and value.

But it should not be forgotten that statistical prediction does not predict for any given individual, but only for the population as a whole.[17] For example, it may have been reliably ascertained that engaged couples from mixed religious backgrounds, say Presbyterian and Roman Catholic, have a 50 percent probability of getting divorced within seven years if they go ahead and get married. But this does not mean that a particular couple with these characteristics who come to a minister for premarital counseling have an even chance of their marriage falling on the rocks. Either they will end in the divorce courts, or they won't. It is precisely the *unique* factors in their situation—including among these the more or less skilled counseling of the minister at this crucial point in their lives—that will affect which way their particular marriage turns out.

In the area of pastoral ministry, clinical pastoral education has traditionally required close scrutiny of verbatim accounts of specific acts of ministry as a central element in its educational method. (And insofar as this no longer holds true, it is to be regretted.) But the published literature on pastoral care is overwhelmingly focused on the commonalities of the major stages, tasks, and crises of life. Just to mention a few titles at random from a well-known series to illustrate the point, one finds volumes on the pastoral care of the dying, of childless couples, of the alcoholic and his family, and so on. Even when a single case is used, as in Becker's *Family Pastoral Care*,[18] it is primarily to illustrate the general principles of this *type* of ministry. Such an approach is obviously valuable, and properly has priority as experts try to provide help to working pastors in what is still, after all, a relatively new field as far as systematic principles are concerned.

Yet this need not be taken to imply that the generalizing study constitutes the only worthwhile method, to the exclusion of other approaches. Indeed, two limitations are immediately apparent. One is the "gaps," occupied by those whose situation or troubles do not readily fall into any general category. Where can one turn, say, for guidance concerning happily married but in some ways frustrated blue-collar workers? Or does one have to wait for the experts to write a book on the pastoral care of expectant parents, or of the "Bobs, Carols, Teds, and Alices" of our congregations? The other limitation of the usual "general characteristics" approach is that it inevitably omits, rather than mines, some of the very uniqueness involved in the situation of any given marrying, dying, grieving, or rejoicing individual.

This is not for a moment to deny the value of having general principles elucidated for rough-and-ready guidance. All

that is being contended is that this is not the only fruitful
method. Nor does the approach proposed in the present volume rest on any suggestion that pastoral care is "an art," with
the obscurantist implication that one cannot really learn anything about it by reading books. (That would be self-defeat-
ing!) By itself, the undisciplined subjectivity of "it just felt
like the right thing to do at the time" is inadequate as the
basis of a pastoral ministry.

In fact, of course, appeal is not being made to purely "private" knowledge. The appraisal and discussion of the situation
and ministry are the author's own. But the verbatim records
of the pastoral relationship, together with the author's own
train of thought in reflecting upon it, are deliberately offered
for public inspection. This is done not merely with awareness
but with appreciation of the fact that other observers may
draw different and even contrary conclusions that will help
to check those presented here. In other words, I am not taking
refuge in the unarguable assertion, "This is how it looks to
me," but openly courting response from other perspectives.

The burden of the present argument is "for" careful attention to the individual case. And it is for it with full recognition
that anything approaching "objective" understanding of particular human situations is not to be expected—at least in the
continued absence of either omniscience or universal telepathy
on our part. Even so, there is no escaping the fact that individual, personal judgment plays a decisive part in a minister's
pastoral caring. The same is true of the historian, the judge,
and the physician in their work. However much help we will
seek and obtain from books or wise counselors in the process,
eventually we *alone* assemble the evidence, draw the inferences, and make a decision as to what to do in the particular
circumstances of any given pastoral relationship.[19]

Therefore, in addition to a grasp of relevant general principles, there is ample reason for careful attention to the very
singularities of the unique situation. Whatever our theories

of pastoral care, whatever "school" of counseling we espouse, we are dead men as far as effective ministry is concerned the moment we cease to be alive to more particular questions. What did I actually accomplish in my relationship with that person? Was it what I set out to do, and if not, what altered my aims or frustrated their realization? What does it mean *to this man* to be dying—granting all that we know about the meaning of dying in general to patients in general?

Gordon Allport has been the most eminent advocate of what can be learned from the single case in psychology. He repeatedly called for serious attention to and appreciation of the richness of human individuality.[20] His little book *Letters from Jenny* is itself a contribution to such an appreciation. Here too, his purpose is primarily to do justice to an individual's uniqueness, without which she cannot be understood, let alone explained.[21]

Since our purpose is the practice of ministry, it is necessary to push the question of the value of the single case a little farther than this. In so doing, we find that there are three separable aspects to the question: value for what? In the first place, what does the mountain of labor involved in writing up verbatims of pastoral conversations and reflecting on them at length have to offer toward the future ministry to the person concerned? To put it another way, is it like taking a harpoon to catch a minnow? Supposing for the moment that the analyses of the ministry to the Jacksons had been made in depth while the ministering was in progress, would they have been potentially valuable in enabling more effective care of the members of the family?

Now there are crucial questions involved here as to whether the methods of reasoning concerning what was going on are valid and whether the results are accurate. Both points could well be argued by the outside observer. Some readers may feel that the reasoning and conclusions are so erroneous that to have operated on the basis of them thereafter would have made for a worse ministry to the Jacksons, not a better one. Subjectively, of course, the author believes that as a result of the analyses he has a better understanding of the family members and their needs as well as of the strengths and weaknesses of his own ministry. But as has been said, we always *do* minister on the basis of our personal assessment of a given situation, be it right or wrong. So only if some of us get more "hung up" and awkward as a result of attempting systematic reflection, would the conclusion be justified that this impedes rather than assists future ministry to the people concerned.

The second and third aspects of the question both concern *the weight of the single case for general principles.* (This also raises crucial philosophical questions, since the weakness of the single case is that it is the extreme case of induction, but it is beyond my competence to launch into a consideration of "inductive probabilities.") The simpler form of the issue concerns the value to the minister involved in his future ministry to other people. For here one party, the minister, "carries over" into new situations. And the things he thinks he has learned, both about his own ministry and about the human situation, will influence him thereafter as he becomes involved in other pastoral relationships that may be more or less similar. It will obviously be crucial to distinguish the nature and the degree of the similarity between one situation and the next, in order to avoid false generalizations. In a real sense, the substantive issues of pastoral care considered in the remainder of this chapter are the author's testimony to what he thinks he learned, by way of new questions or partial answers, for more general principles from his ministry to the Jacksons.

Finally, in its most hazardous form, the question is what value the single case and one man's experience can have for others who are involved in ministering to yet other people in different situations. For here there is no direct carry-over at all. Insofar as the author's primary concern is to propose and demonstrate a method that he has himself found of value in the hope that others may adopt it to the benefit of their own ministering, the book does not stand or fall on the answer to this question. Nevertheless, the reader's considered response to the remainder of this chapter will point to a preliminary answer. If something of the content of what is discussed is illuminating and helpful, and it happens to be a point raised by the verbatim material, this will be a testimony to at least the suggestive value of the single case. Moreover, there is something of a "heads I win, tails you lose" argument here too! For even if this present case has nothing to offer, it remains conceivable that a more adequate case and/or interpretation might be more productive.

## ROLE PROBLEMS

It is time to pass from problems of method to substantive matters. The first set of issues to be discussed, because aspects of them are at stake in the relationship with the Jacksons and seem to arise quite frequently in pastoral care, can be conveniently grouped under the heading of "role problems." Within this general category are three issues that will be touched on.

The first concerns the shift from informal to formal relationships.[22] Back in the late '50s, Wayne Oates used to hand out a mimeographed sheet in his introductory pastoral care and counseling course that distinguished between informal, formal, and confused relationships. By informal relationships, he meant those in which one's role as a minister is either unknown or inactive, such as anonymous relationships, social relationships, and family relationships. The category of formal relationships comprises those in which, both in one's own mind and that of the person with whom one is speaking, one's role as a minister is activated. Confused relationships, against which he was warning us to be on our guard, occur when one

For those who regard it as important to further the ability of all church members to offer caring, helping relationships, this would seem to increase the significance of the problem. So would an inclination to the view that most people are engaged in a continual process of coping and finding resources for coping that only in the event of failure will move toward levels of dysfunction and overt seeking of formal professional help. Sensitivity at this point would be a valuable approach to fostering positive mental health at an earlier stage in the process and therefore more desirable than usual. At the point where the "one being looked to as a helper" becomes aware of this and that he has been missing the boat up to now, there is a little research evidence that is useful. It has been shown that when there is a breakdown in the communication system in therapy because of dissimilar expectations on the part of the participants, the most helpful procedure is discussion and clarification of the role expectations of both parties.[25] This would seem likely to be applicable to the less technical situation at issue here. But its usefulness would be limited to rectifying the breakdown of a relationship stemming from role confusion after it had occurred. How to prevent such breakdowns is less clear.

The second aspect of role problems meriting some thought might be termed that of "territorial rights" to appropriate a term from that currently most "in" of fields, ecology. For during the period covered by the case material, there were three professional helpers, with related and overlapping areas of concern and competence, all involved with Mrs. Jackson at once.

Given that this *was* the situation, some consultation between those involved for the purpose of mutual clarification of goals and of ways and means would seem to have been desirable—and a little took place. Mrs. Jackson's priest and I discussed the situation on a number of occasions. In retrospect, at least, there seems to have been an implicit division of dominant perspectives, to use Hiltner's terms.[26] The priest's ministry was

tries to activate one's ministerial role inappropriately or wit
out clarification, e.g., in relation to one's own wife, or when
person with whom you have had a social relationship begi
to speak to you as a minister and you do not catch on. I ha
not been able to find the whole schema in print, althou
Oates has described four factors that have to be brought in
focus in order to establish a secure counseling relationship

It is precisely at the point of the desirability of a shift
a hitherto prevailing type of relationship that there seems
be the need for further exploration, particularly with respe
to a shift from an informal to a formal relationship. For  
ample, with Mrs. Jackson my primary relationship was that
a professional colleague. But, although answered in the ne
tive in Chapter I, an important question is whether I h
failed to perceive earlier attempts on her part to have  
relate to her as a minister, before she was hospitalized. T
problem is certainly remarkably common in the verbatims t
our seminary students bring back from their summers as s
dent assistants in congregations. They are constantly surpris
to find themselves in the middle of a pastoral conversati
after what had started out as an innocent informal relationsh
Sometimes they fail to catch the attempted transition on  
part of the other person altogether. Almost invariably they
very late in doing so.

A hunch would be that this is least likely to be a probl
in a relationship between a minister and a member of his c
gregation—although not nonexistent even there, especially
those ministers who do not invariably maintain a "professic
distance." [24] It is more likely for a minister to be insensit
to a tentative reaching out for help from a fellow ministe
other colleague. It is certainly difficult for the minister's v
drinking a cup of coffee with a friend, or an elder talking v
a church member, promptly to pick up the transition f
casual conversation to a help-seeking approach on the par
the other person.

chiefly from a dominant organizing perspective, and he mobilized the congregation to provide some very effective help for this family in its chaotic turmoil. By the nature of my own position and the good fortune of being able to rely on the priest's active ministry, I was almost necessarily limited to a shepherding perspective in relation to whichever member of the family happened to be hospitalized at the time. Also Father Dawson probably regarded me as having greater competence in "counseling" than he himself did. (He did not get to read the verbatims!) In addition to this, I spoke to the psychiatrist on the telephone a couple of times, to obtain his appraisal of the prognosis for Mrs. Jackson. The psychiatrist was amiable enough, but did not evince any particular interest in what "the other members of the team" might be contributing to the overall situation.

This was the given situation, then. But the question that has next to be asked is: Is this setup positively desirable, merely defensible, or quite deplorable? What is there to be said for having several overlapping, but not really cooperative if not actually competitive, ministries going on at the same time? [27] (It is appreciated that this may not be exactly a burning issue for those ministers in rural areas who have to serve their people in every capacity from wise man to witch doctor!) The situation with Mr. Jackson was somewhat different of course in that the very possibility of my relating to him as I did rested heavily on the fact that others were already doing what *had* to be done in practical terms.

Even the criteria that should be applied in attempting to answer this question are difficult to determine. "Prior claim" in and of itself—in the sense that "I was helping her first"— should probably count for little or nothing, even though occasionally a belligerent minister will explicitly invoke it and tell a chaplain to keep his hands off "his" parishioner. On the other hand, special expertise should clearly be an important consideration. Yet what is to be done in a situation like the Jacksons' where some kind of family therapy might seem indicated as the preferred mode of treatment, but the "expert," in the person of the psychiatrist, is committed to a one-to-one approach? Another tack in attempting to answer the question would be to take the line that the patient, the one seeking help, should have the final say. Implicitly, this is what happened in the present case, with Mrs. Jackson opting for all three helpers at once. If it had been left up to the helping professionals themselves to decide, there would not have been unanimity, nor even any clear guidelines by which to arrive at a decision.

To try to be more positive about it, one kind of criterion that obviously must count for a great deal is the "therapeutic,"—the good of the patient. But this is almost circular, for who is to decide? Psychiatrists have generally tended to take over the medical model, of one doctor in charge, with freedom to call in consultants if he feels it necessary or is hard pressed by the patient. But then with a refreshing willingness to question what has been taken for granted, Bernard Steinzor has doubted whether this is really an appropriate model. "Who is to decide which professional is helping the patient more at any particular time? So why not . . . encourage a patient to discuss his problems with any professional leader he wishes to consult?" He notes that two of the usual objections to this are that a patient would play off one counselor against the other, and that he would avoid painful problems by claiming to have discussed them with the other therapist. But Steinzor discounts these arguments when weighed against the advantages to the patient of coming to realize that he cannot learn everything from one teacher, and thus moving toward a more rational assumption of the responsibility for directing his own life.[28]

Steinzor has made a strong case that therapeutic benefit to the patient is not necessarily optimally guaranteed by the medical model. But it would seem that *economic*, as well as therapeutic considerations, must weigh heavily on the minister. Mrs. Jackson was willing to have all three professionals engaged in helping her, and it is conceded that that may well have offered the maximum chance of health for her. Similarly, Mr. Jackson basks in the warm relationship offered him by the chaplain, perhaps even using it as a sort of emotional stroking that he can afford to indulge in precisely because the committee is seeing to more pressing realities. But what of the many, many other people in need? The problem of priorities is, like that of the poor, always with us. But the author, at least, finds it harder to justify spending considerable time with someone who has other help available, all other things being equal. Certainly, the chaplain's job description emphasized ministry to those far from home or without a current church association, and quite appropriately so.

In short, this discussion is not intended to discount the value for Mrs. Jackson of both working directly on her problem with the psychiatrist in his office and sharing some of her concerns with those who live and work around her who could surround her with support and loving concern. It is, however, to bring to the forefront from one particular angle, the basic question: Should I be ministering here, and if so, why? [29]

Finally, there is a third issue within the general rubric of role problems that is worth considering: a different facet of the above concern over the relation between various healing ministries. Assuming that a minister and a doctor each has a valid and distinct ministry to a particular patient, it would seem important to make a distinction between cooperative and complementary functioning. There has been so much emphasis on doctor-clergy cooperation, "the healing team," and "interdisciplinary ministries" of late, that these catch-phrases begin to ring bells like "motherhood" and "apple pie"! So much is this so that it is possible to find induced the feeling that one is letting down the side if one is not in constant communication with the medical members of the team.

In some situations active consultation and cooperation may be highly desirable—as for instance in a joint attack on the physical, emotional, and spiritual problems involved in rehabilitation. The person who is struggling to rebuild a new

life after a major heart attack or the loss of a leg faces such
a complex process of readjustment in building a radically new
life-style that it may well be beneficial for the doctor and the
minister to coordinate their efforts. But earlier, say when that
massive coronary erupted, complementary ministries were
called for. The physician would have been watching the patient's vital signs like a hawk in the intensive care unit. The
patient's survival is his primary concern and responsibility,
and a minister hanging around for more than a minute or two
would just get under his feet. But at the same time the pastor
has an important ministry of his own to the stricken family in
this upheaval. This, then, is a plea for discrimination: is a
given situation such that the extra work of active cooperation
is desirable, or should each professional simply get on with
his own, complementary, ministry?

The problem with theoretically complementary ministries,
of course, is that in practice they may not be! It would have
been quite possible for the estimate made by each of those
involved with Mrs. Jackson to have differed radically—and
thus for the "course of treatment" pursued on the basis of
each appraisal of the situation to have been at cross-purposes
with the others. This happens in the parish, too, when the
pastor's informed sensitivity regarding the grief process and
the "grief work" that needs to be accomplished is undone by
the well-meaning neighbors who urge the bereft widower not
to cry, to be brave, to have a strong faith. Ultimately the recip-
ient of "help" has to decide to whom to listen—and he may
not always make the wise choice!

## PROBLEMS WITH A ROGERIAN APPROACH

The next cluster of issues to be raised bears in various ways
on the question of desirable methods and problems of technique in pastoral conversations and counseling. The issues

relate primarily to Carl Rogers' "client-centered" approach.[30] Rogers' influence on pastoral care theory was dominant, even overwhelming, for almost twenty years following the Second World War. More recently the proliferation of schools of therapy has begun to make its influence felt, as evidenced by Clinebell's consideration of no less than seventeen different approaches for pastoral use.[31] Accordingly, the pastoral conversations recorded in the first three chapters could be analyzed from a number of other theoretical standpoints. But this would disproportionately expand the scope of the present section. Moreover, as already avowed in the introduction, the author still places considerable stock in the client-centered approach—certainly in preference to any single alternative. This does not mean that there are not a number of serious questions to be raised though.

In the first place, there is a simple practical observation. I have heard early pastoral advocates of Rogers' approach emphasize its short-term effectiveness, in addition to its nontechnical nature and the fact that it is difficult for a minister to do active harm this way.[32] The possibility of accomplishing something worthwhile in a mere six counseling sessions was an obvious attraction to the busy pastor. But it is now open to serious doubt how far this supposed advantage holds true. There are cases on record of Carl Rogers' own counseling running into the twelfth month on a twice-a-week basis, and of running over eighty-five sessions.[33] Inasmuch as the same tendency to take longer and longer has also characterized the practice of psychoanalysis, one cannot but wonder whether it will not also become the case with some of the newer options such as behavior therapy and transactional analysis.

This much, at least, is plain then: the general need for a minister to limit himself to something less than a dozen counseling sessions because of his other commitments no longer automatically indicates the Rogerian approach as the method of choice. Mr. Jackson, for instance, made no move to utilize the facilitative relationship to work on his difficulties. After allowing for the drawbacks of brevity and medication, there was no particular reason to suppose that he would have begun to do so given a few more conversations. Yet this is not to claim that more "directive" methods are a *quicker* way of "getting to the root of the trouble," an assumption that Rogers has been concerned to dispute.

A more critical problem, with both practical and theoretical aspects, is that of *consistency*. The client-centered approach is based on unconditional positive regard for the client and empathetic understanding of how the immediate world looks and feels to him, these attitudes being conveyed by "reflection." Yet it is evident that very few ministers are thoroughly trained and skilled therapists. Accordingly, it is most unlikely that the minister will be able to maintain these attitudes through thick and thin. Probably it will more often be the case, as in the conversations with Mrs. Jackson, that some of the responses will manifest these qualities and other remarks will fail to, and may even work in the opposite direction.

In fact, there is even evidence suggesting that no less an expert in this approach than Carl Rogers himself is not consistent! In one scrutinized case, at least, he seems to have shown more empathy and warmth when the client was developing insight and discrimination than when the client was blocking or anxious.[34] Further, research by Rogers and his colleagues has shown that other Rogerian therapists likewise fail to maintain the level of "the therapeutic conditions" constant over the course of therapy with schizophrenics.[35]

The basic question would seem to be: How important is it to be absolutely consistent? Is it undeviating warmth and empathy that the counselee needs to perceive in order to derive benefit from counseling, or is it enough for these attitudes to "come through" to him most of the time? It seems to be generally held that children learn to cope and adapt much better in relation to, say, steadily harsh parents, than parents who are lovey-dovey one minute and cold or rejecting the next. What, then, is the effect on the unfortunate parishioner if he accurately picks up a fumbling and inconsistent approach on the part of the minister? Would it perhaps be better for those whose ability genuinely to embody the attitudes advocated by client-centered therapy with reasonable consistency is severely limited, not to try it at all? [36]

Before this is too quickly conceded, one more piece of evidence has to be taken into account. The finding that Rogerian therapists are not consistently Rogerian was derived from judges' ratings of segments of the tape recordings of therapy sessions. But in addition to this, both the patients and the therapists filled out "relationship inventories" at various points in the course of the therapy. And both the therapists and the patients perceived or felt the conditions of the relationship to have been much more stable and consistent throughout than they "in fact" seem to have been. This does suggest that those involved tend to appraise a relationship on a rather broad gauge more than on the basis of particular responses.[37]

The question posed by Truax in his research was "whether Rogers is consistent, as he claims, or whether he uses differential reinforcement." [38] Whatever the answer given to the consistency problem, this seems to point to an even more fundamental issue between client-centered theory and learning theories. Rogers firmly espouses reflective empathy, and as a basic tenet holds that denying negative feelings and fears (or positive ones for that matter) is undesirable. In learning theory, on the other hand, the concept of "reinforcement" is stressed as a pervasive influence in human development and change. So there are conflicting opinions as to what would happen, given the most consistent reflection imaginable.

Accurate empathetic reflection is perhaps not reinforcement in the strict technical sense—but the question at stake is whether it is perceived as such or operates analogously. If so, what are the consequences of uniform reinforcement "across the board"? Does this lead to a *divergence* of feelings—becoming more happy about whatever a person is happy about, and more sad with respect to those things he feels bad about? In the above form, the questions are too abstract and technical for the writer to be capable of answering them adequately and for the average reader to care. But the form in which they make themselves felt in practice cannot so easily be dismissed.

It must be a fairly common experience for most ministers to have striven to reflect the feelings of a parishioner, only to have that person wallow deeper in them—particularly depressive feelings! One remembers all too well the way it goes. The parishioner says: "I feel pretty bad today." And the minister tries to come back with a faithful reflection of the feelings that are being expressed: "You're not feeling so good." And the patient agrees: "No, I'm not. I feel terrible." And the minister picks it up: "You really are feeling low and blue." And the parishioner almost clutches/hugs his misery: "Yes. I feel absolutely ghastly." So it goes on, *ad nauseam!* We have heard and believed that it is inappropriate to attempt to cheer such a person up, to minimize or brush aside the gloom with stress on the bright side ("count your blessings"), to try to change the subject to distract him from the train of thought and get his mind off it, or to offer premature reassurance. Yet especially perhaps with those inclined to be depressive, there seems to be a real problem. Without any unrealistic confidence in trying to talk them out of it, one can still be dubious about reflection serving to do anything but push them deeper into it!

The solution might seem to lie with differential diagnosis. Rogers himself forthrightly denies that one kind of symptom, one form of dysfunction needs one kind of therapy, while a different "illness" needs another kind of treatment, and holds that a medical model is not valid. He claims that the necessary and sufficient conditions of effective therapy are universal: "diagnostic knowledge is not essential to psychotherapy." The best recent critical appraisal of the controlled research evidence known to this author neither supports nor denies this contention. It does demolish the well-publicized myth that no psychotherapy is any more effective than simply being on a waiting list for treatment, or the passage of time along. While admitting that it does begin to look as if systematic desensitization may be more effective with some phobias and specific focalized anxieties, the main conclusion is that "there is hardly any evidence that one traditional school of psychotherapy yields a better outcome than another. In fact, the question has hardly been put to a fair test." [39]

Abstractly, perhaps, differential diagnosis commends itself both as a commonsense solution and an elegant one. But even if it should be proved to have merit, it is in any case a fiendishly difficult task. For what are the criteria for determining which approach should be used on a particular occasion? Does it depend on the nature of the "real," basic, underlying problem—and how is the average minister going to ascertain this anyway? Or are the minister's own temperament, inclinations, and skills more important factors?

At this crucial point Clinebell is less helpful than one could wish, despite his stimulating sketch of so many alternative approaches for pastoral use.[40] His basic thesis, of course, is that pastoral counseling is a helping function which requires a variety of methods. And at this point he continues: "To minister to the varied needs of those who seek his help, the pastor must be able to shift gears in his counseling—to utilize approaches which are appropriate to the needs, resources, problems, and limitations of each person. *He must be able to utilize different facets of his personality freely and flexibly.*" [41] Here he is saying in general terms that the choice of an approach must be guided both by the minister's self-appraisal and by his perception of the needs of the other—though judging by the italics, the emphasis is on the former. Yet Clinebell clearly expects the minister to be able to diagnose the nature and depth of the person's problems in living, for the purposes of

differential treatment.[42] And when he spells out the basic criterion, not for choosing between the seventeen methods, but
for making the simpler decision as to "whether a particular
person is more apt to be helped by supportive or uncovering
counseling methods," this criterion resides in the other person.
"The most useful criterion is *the person's degree of ego
strength.* Those with weak, rigid or defective ego development
do not respond to uncovering, insight-oriented approaches." [43]
He lists a number of characteristics indicative of the presence
of ego weakness, and also states that this is usually involved
in alcoholics, drug addicts, the overt or borderline psychotic,
the chronically depressed or delinquent or dependent, and
those with multiple psychosomatic problems.[44]

There are no easy answers. Indeed, it is obvious from the
internecine warfare of psychologists, psychotherapists, psy-
choanalysts, and counselors of every hue and persuasion that
the "science" of helping people by listening, talk, or action is
in its infancy still. The most that the author can presume to do
is to share his own theoretical stance and some of the reasoning that lies behind it, in approaching the issues from yet another angle.

## Pastoral Authority

There are two reasons for treating the issue of pastoral authority here. The first is that one small aspect of it is raised
by the case material at two points. Mrs. Jackson, close to the
end of our first long conversation, stated that she certainly felt
better since she gave up trying to do it all and came into the
hospital for a rest, inasmuch as she has a very leaning family.
And my response (31) was: "Yes, and *you* need to be able to
share the burden at times—if not with your family, then with
your pastor or chaplain or someone." Here, then, is an authoritative prescriptive statement, the nature of which we shall
examine in a moment. A milder version of the same thing is

referred to in the introduction to Chapter II, when I wonder
aloud whether it may be necessary for her to live apart from
her family, at least temporarily.

The main reason for this section, however, is to continue
and conclude the discussion at the end of the previous section,
but from a different frame of reference. For the appropriate
use of pastoral authority constitutes my own solution to the
question of when to depart from purely Rogerian methods.
Having raised so many questions about this, I would be irre-
sponsible not to sketch my personal position, even though it
does not solve all the difficulties. To attempt to encapsulate
it in such brief compass is somewhat ludicrous, but considerable expansion of the argument may be found elsewhere.[45]

Three definitions are needed to begin with. The term "authority in pastoral care" is used as an inclusive term. It covers
all the kinds and aspects of authority that are operative in
pastoral care relationships—the latter being defined as those
relationships where the focus is on the good of the parishion-
er(s). The general authority of the minister by virtue of his
call, ordination, representative capacity, and other roles vis-à-
vis the parishioner falls within it so far as any or all of these
elements color his pastoral ministry. Any particular church
member's idiosyncratic perception of the minister's authority,
whatever has gone into making this up, is a factor. And so is
the minister's own conception of an attempted exercise of his
authority as this is mediated by his personality.

The term "pastoral authority" is reserved for that aspect or
kind of authority peculiarly appropriate to, or distinctively
exercised in pastoral care. This is identified with "the introduction by the minister of Christian truths and norms in their
unique application to the specific life-situation of the other
person in the pastoral relationship." [46] That verbal behavior of
this kind is peculiarly and directly an expression of "pastoral
authority" is maintained on four basic grounds. "(1) The
Christian truths and principles to which such verbalizations
primarily refer are regarded as normative, nominally at least,

by ministers and church members alike. (2) Parishioners formally recognize the minister as in some sense the representative of the Christian position, by training, by calling from God and the congregation, and by role. (3) Historically, this category of expression has been an important and characteristic part of the ministry of the care of souls. (4) The 'authority' of the ordained minister, according to Reformed doctrine, is very closely linked, if not identified with, his right and duty to administer the Word of God." [47]

The third definition is of "obedience" as the appropriate response to the exercise of pastoral authority—for the latter is always relational and dynamic. "Obedience" must be understood in its root meaning of to hear, to listen, without the debased overtones of "to knuckle under." [48] Therefore pastoral authority as properly correlative to obedience means the right to be listened to attentively and seriously, but not necessarily to be "obeyed." What is being strongly upheld by this definition is the possibility of the simultaneous existence of pastoral authority and of noncompliance by the church member in a constructive relationship. [49]

Within this framework, both my prescriptive recommendation that Mrs. Jackson find people with whom she can share her burden and my raising the possibility that she may need to live alone for a while fall readily into place. These are instances of the minister's authority in pastoral care, in that they are professional judgments based on some training and competence in psychological matters. Perhaps the commonest example of this kind of expertise would be the increasingly general awareness of ministers of the well-documented importance of "grief work" in bereavement situations. Any competent minister will seek to assist a person to grieve adequately at the rupture or termination of a meaningful relationship, by explicit encouragement if necessary. This is to exercise appropriate authority in pastoral care, but not "pastoral authority."

The placement given to my advice to Mrs. Jackson has not dealt with the fact that this is already a departure from a purely Rogerian approach. This issue will now have to be treated at greater length. My position is that the client-centered approach is indispensable to responsible pastoral ministry, but not always sufficient to it. Listening to the other person, trying to understand how the world looks and feels to him, and communicating that understanding to him in the context of steady positive regard, constitute the vital and often lengthy preliminaries to anything else. Preliminaries, indeed, is a misleading word if it is taken to imply that there has been total and irremediable failure if progress is not made beyond this point in the relationship with any given person.

But it is held that if the need is there and the occasion is promising, the special contribution of pastoral care is to make explicit the relation between the gospel and principles of the Christian faith on the one hand and the life and circumstances of the individual parishioner on the other. As one example only, suppose that a church member has an overall commitment to Christ as his Lord, but that a particular segment of his present behavior—let's say, an increasingly inappropriate involvement with his secretary—runs counter to this. The contention here is that, given a good pastoral relationship, failure to point out the discrepancy may be as great, if not as obvious, a failure as launching into condemnation at the outset.

There is a corollary, however, concerning the appropriateness of the response to any such exercise of pastoral authority. This should be measured in terms, not of a compliance-rejection dimension, but of whether it is automatic or considered. The desirable response is a considered one—regardless of which way it goes. Over the latter the minister has no control. The man may opt in favor of his secretary over his wife and for his Christian commitment to resolve the dissonance, once the matter has been brought out into the open.

This is to approach from a different perspective the problem of when to depart from Rogers. Clinebell's starting point is the same as that adumbrated here: "The Rogerian method provides a firm foundation but not the entire edifice of an adequate approach to counseling." [50] But he develops his argument by calling for diagnosis on the basis of psychological factors, principally ego strength, for the purpose of determining which of a number of counseling methods to employ. This falls within "authority in pastoral care" in my terms, and obviously I am not against it. In certain situations such as bereavement I would hope to be able to take the universality of minimal psychological competence for granted. However, I strongly suspect that the average parish minister's psychological expertise is and will remain rather limited, inasmuch as he is a general practitioner with another area of primary concern.

The criterion for departure from Rogers' theory that I am advocating is the determination that specifically pastoral care and counseling is called for on religious or theological grounds. And pastoral authority has been identified with relating the Christian gospel to the individual's unique situation. For this is the main area of the parish minister's competence. Yet unlike other professionals, the minister's authority does not rest on the possession of a body of esoteric knowledge that he holds in common only with his fellow ministers. Every church member has the responsibility to be conversant with the Scriptures, which in any case he hears read and interpreted at services of worship. So what is the function or purpose of the exercise of pastoral authority by the ordained minister? Is it to remind the parishioner of that which he is presumed to have forgotten, to instruct him where he is ignorant, to interpret a specific application to a novel situation where he is unimaginative?

From a psychological standpoint, the rationale lies in the human penchant for self-deception and rationalization. This is held to justify exerting "pressure toward cognitive balance" on those who are psychologically relatively free to respond, in order to end such rationalization.[51] Nor is this foreign to the doctrinal understanding in Reformed theology that every Christian is at the same time redeemed and a sinner. This includes the minister, of course, so that his right and responsibility to exercise pastoral authority is always fraught with the potential for distortion and misuse. But it is to emphasize that no Christian is beyond the need of the help of his brother, as well as and as a means of the help of the Holy Spirit. And the implication is clearly of the reciprocal right of all church members to exercise pastoral authority, not only with respect to one another but also vis-à-vis the minister.[52]

Several factors, such as role expectations and individual personality, that will influence the decision as to whether to risk the exercise of pastoral authority are noted in the larger study.[53] But without doubt, it could be employed *more effectively* if the nature of an appropriate response to its exercise were generally understood. Ministers would be prepared to "have their say" and then to leave the parishioner completely free to act as he chooses after serious consideration of what had been said to him. Church members would feel genuinely unconstrained by any directional response expectations. They would not feel that their relationship with the minister or standing in the congregation hung in the balance. So they could wrestle with what had been said to them before God, and the likelihood of a mature response would be enhanced considerably.

Undoubtedly there is an element of "risk" involved in the exercise of pastoral authority. But it is not, as commonly thought, that the minister will lose some of his authority if the parishioner does not comply with what he has said. The risk is that the minister's Christian understanding, whether of the gospel or of the church member, may be inadequate or just plain wrong. It is the risk implicit in fallible human diagnosis, even on our own theological grounds, without the aid of the instruments and procedures of the modern medical laboratory.

It is the potential harm that can be wrought by an ill-timed incision, or a slip of the pastor's scalpel. It is these risks which must give pause—yet without so unnerving the minister that when to the best of his knowledge and belief the operation is vital he continues to hide behind merely palliative measures.

# V

# PASTORAL THEOLOGY

The double task of this final chapter is an attempt to uphold the validity and demonstrate the potential value of "pastoral theology." This will be a more purely theoretical exercise, though it is not simply "academic" in the debased sense of being without any practical consequences or important. The reader is forewarned that it may seem rather heavy going. It is a little difficult to break down the habits of a lifetime of British reserve and come across with the fervor of an evangelist; nor does the subject matter lend itself readily to such a style. Nevertheless, to the author this chapter constitutes not something of the order of an optional extra, but the heart of the matter.

## METHODOLOGY

The first requirement is to attempt to *justify* "pastoral theology" as a form of theology. This was not a problem involved in what was done in the first three chapters. There was no reason to expect serious argument about the validity of trying to analyze pastoral encounters from a theological perspective.

There may be sincere doubts about the *usefulness* of the procedure, on the basis of the time it takes. Reservations about the direction in which the analysis proceeded are to be expected from many quarters of theological conviction. But a flat assertion that such a process is illegitimate is unlikely to arise from within the church. For all that was proposed and engaged in in those chapters was an operational procedure, a way of thinking about some pastoral conversations that might possibly shed more light on what happened. The crux of the matter was the use of theology to inform pastoral care. But in any case, our Christian beliefs largely motivate our pastoral care, and color what is done to a greater or lesser extent. So deliberately using them to analyze what had already been done was not so very different.

At this juncture, we come to the counterpoint! For what is being upheld is *the use of pastoral care for theology*. That is, the intention is to try to make a case for "pastoral theology" as Hiltner used the term—reflections on aspects of the life and work of the church as valid contributions to the task of constructive theology.[54] At this point, it would be ostrich-like not to expect to have a fight on one's hands.

It should be noted, however, that this is an internal fight, arising within the fellowship of believing Christians. If the purpose of the later sections of this chapter were to make a definitive statement about human pride, or hope and despair, or dependency, then it would have to speak convincingly to philosophers, psychologists, and others, and the problems would be larger still.[55] But given what is being attempted here, the problem revolves around the decision as to *what is the nature and source of legitimate evidence* for a theological statement that proposes to say something from the Christian perspective.

Historically, theologians have looked to the Bible or the church, or sometimes to Christian experience. One, or some combination, of these has been accepted as the test and guarantee of any theological affirmation. Moreover, for the most part these sources have been regarded as complete, final, and infallible. Williams has called this the "confessional type" of theological method, which makes of something unique in Christian experience—be it faith, Scriptures, or the pope—the ultimate court of appeal.[56] The Reformers themselves, while they challenged the then established "authoritative source" of theological truth, never doubted that there *was* such a source for the solution of the problems of faith, life, and order.[57]

Thus, if "Reformed theology" is held to be inextricably bound to the confessional method, this essay is beyond the pale. As it is, the writer does attach great importance to the accumulated witness of the believing community—to the Scriptures, and to the theology and tradition of the church. But the position taken here is that there is no accessible source of theological truth that is completely authoritative. Modern scholarship has demonstrated the limitations of the traditional "standards," without denuding them of all their importance. The new hermeneutic has established the inevitability of the interpretative element in their actual content: "There is no uninterpreted revelation." [58] And the ubiquity of interpretation entails an ever-open door to finitude and fallibility, not to mention sinfulness, on the part of the interpreter. In any case, the "special standards" suffer from the additional limitation that they are not exhaustive sources of information on every issue of importance to Christians. Consequently, in addition to the intrinsic interpretation, inferences and deductions from general principles to concrete problems have continually to be made. From the foregoing argument, it is obvious that the author aligns himself with the "rational type" of theological method, of which Williams writes:

The rational type accepts the uniqueness of the Christian faith and perspective; but it holds that Christian

> beliefs are corrigible by what is discovered through the
> meeting of the Christian perspective with the experi-
> ence and conceptions imbedded in other perspectives.
> From this viewpoint faith, regeneration, revelation,
> Bible, and creed are conditions of the discovery of
> the full truth of Christianity; but are not self-authenti-
> cating criteria of truth.[59]

This position requires a corresponding openness to *any
evidence* that might possibly be relevant, whatever its source.
Otherwise theologizing is in danger of becoming an exercise
resembling the court-martial of Colonel Billy Mitchell in the
1920's.[60] All the evidence that really mattered at that time was
about the need to improve the United States Air Force. But
this was not the formal issue before the court, and it was ruled
inadmissible. By selectively defining the specified charges, it
was possible to dismiss as irrelevant to the case in hand what,
to any impartial and intelligent observer, was clearly the vital
issue. The analogy is precise, and the warning clear. The outcome of that piece of official stupidity was Pearl Harbor. It
may be no less drastic for theology.

As has been pointed out, the verdict of most theologians
down the centuries would have been that no data from the
actual practice of pastoral care—let alone from areas of "secular" knowledge—could possibly alter the Christian "facts"
about a given subject, ascertained from Biblical and confessional sources. Thus it is the use of traditionally extracurricu-
lar sources of evidence, not only for raising questions for theology to answer but of actually contributing to the theological
answers themselves, that has to be supported. For this is still
commonly rejected. Tillich's stated method of correlation, for
example, allowed existential situations to raise questions, but
understood the answers to these questions as coming from
theological sources alone.[61] And Tom Oden, who is becoming
a prolific contributor in our field, holds that the only way in
which anything theological can be said about current ideas

and practices in or outside of the church is by the application of the *analogia fidei* to such theories or practices.[62]

Up to this point, "pastoral theology" has been defended largely on negative grounds. The proposal to admit pastoral evidence to the task of constructive theology has been supported by denying that the more traditional sources are definitive, in the sense either of complete, or of infallible. But *on positive theological grounds,* too, it is contended that pastoral relationships are a potentially valuable source of evidence for theology. For they reveal, in Boisen's now-famous phrase, "the living human documents." This is affirmed on the basis of the author's belief in God's continuing creative and redemptive activity through the Holy Spirit.[63]

The label "natural theology" is thus rejected insofar as this denotes the achievement of saving knowledge of God (and his purposes in and through the church) by the unaided power of human reason. What *is* claimed is the possibility of knowledge of God's ways in relation to men, from many sources in this world, simply because the God who was incarnate in Christ Jesus, the God of Moses, Paul, and Wesley, continues to be actively engaged in and related to his world and his children.

It has already been noted that, *whatever* the source of information, there is always the problem of distinguishing God's revelation of his relationship with us from the limitations and distortions of our understanding of it. Possibly this poses an even harder task of discrimination with respect to ongoing events, persons, and relationships in our world than it does with regard to the "special standards" of Scriptures and creeds.[64] But the difference is surely one of degree, not of kind. And the difficulties do not, per se, invalidate the attempt in advance. They only argue for great care, tentative inferences, continual concern for eyes of faith, and developed criteria and skills for such discernment.

Indirectly, the present plea for pastoral theology is also buttressed by Jaroslav Pelikan's recent little book, *Development of Christian Doctrine*. Pelikan is in agreement with the Roman Catholic scholar John Courtney Murray that, like it or not, *development of Christian doctrine has undeniably taken place*.[65] And while some of the development that took place was simply a systematizing of what was in Scripture, this was not always the case. Particularly apropos is his statement:

> As later chapters in this book will seek to document, the development of Christian doctrine has not been a unilinear progress, but has been characterized by an openness simultaneously to the past and to the present, while heresy has attempted either to absolutize a particular stage in the development or to sacrifice continuity to relevance.[66]

Pelikan points out that Christian doctrines, while they are ideas and concepts having an inner logic in their evolution, are also *more* than that. In his own words: "The 'inner logic' in the evolution of doctrine must be discerned, therefore, in the matrix of the total life of the Christian community." For "Christian doctrine is what the Church believes, teaches, confesses, as it prays and suffers, serves and obeys, celebrates and awaits the coming of the kingdom of God. It is also an expression of the broken state of Christian faith and witness." [67] In tracing the development that *has* occurred in three specific doctrines, Pelikan shows very clearly how intricately involved the actual life and practice of the church was in the whole process. The history of salvation *since* the New Testament has been very influential in the development that has taken place. The total life of the Christian community has been the matrix in which it has happened. And more specifically, pastoral situations have sometimes been the triggering or precipitating events that led to it.[68]

Returning to the immediate thesis, it has already been acknowledged that what Williams has called the "rational" theological method is espoused. But for present purposes it is only a limited aspect of this method that has to be granted as legitimate, namely, the value of evidence, not from the whole range of "secular" knowledge, but from pastoral operations themselves. Against this, however, have to be set the limitations of the material to hand: its relative brevity, and the distortions introduced by imperfect ministry. Moreover, there are the two more serious problems, of the weight to be attached to a single case, which has already been partially treated in the previous chapter, and also the question of the accuracy and reliability of the theological analyses that have been made. Nevertheless, for all the specific problems, certain possibilities can be clarified.

In principle, there would seem to be three positions that might be taken by those open to the possibility of "pastoral theology" in some sense of the term. There are three "levels" at which theological reflection on concrete pastoral relationships might be held to have value for theology in general—value that remains over and above the benefits for the individual pastor and the specific ministry.

First, a case might be held to have potential *illustrative value* only. This would be the minimal positive level. It would be to hold, for example, that case material might offer support for Reinhold Niebuhr's exposition of the Christian understanding of pride as against Carl Rogers' position, say, and be a valid piece of supportive evidence in the debate.[69]

Second, the theological analysis of a pastoral situation might be held to have *question-raising value*. This is not meant simply in the sense of Tillich's existential question which raises a problem for theology to answer. More pointedly than that, the pastoral data could be considered to have sufficient significance to throw light on a one-sidedness, or limitation, or gap, in a hitherto accepted traditional doctrine by presenting evidence to the contrary.[70] This is the other side of the coin to the illustrative value conceived of as the minimal positive use.

It is to be open to taking a concrete case seriously even when it does *not* agree with a prior systematic position—to treat it in its own right, as perhaps having *corrective* value.

The third and most extreme claim is that pastoral encounters, when wrestled with theologically, have, at least potentially, the capacity for *supplying answers*, supplementing or emending traditional doctrinal statements. (In the nature of the individual case it will never afford total coverage of a doctrine and all its ramifications.) This third position holds that sufficiently strong, almost irrefutable, empirical evidence could do more than merely point to the need for correction of a hitherto accepted articulation of a doctrine. It could actually have constructive value, positively contributing to a more adequate reformulation.

The remainder of this chapter will consist of three attempts to do some second-stage pastoral theology—bringing the theological analyses of the conversations that were made in the first three chapters into dialogue with some systematic doctrinal statements. Once again let it be stated that the theological analyses themselves were made inductively on the basis of the author's theological understandings and positions at that time, and *prior to* any reference back to the confessions and literature of the Christian faith. It is also worth repeating the reminder that the failure of this "mini-case" to contribute anything new would not of itself refute the possibility that another case, another theological analysis might do so (though this possibility can never be "proved"). But it would have been cowardly not to try it and see how it comes out!

## PRIDE

Without ever having read *The Nature and Destiny of Man*, the author had a strong impression from other theological reading that this would be *the* source to turn to for an analysis of human pride as the root of sin.[71] A consulting of this work uncovered that Niebuhr's stated purpose was even more closely applicable to the present task than could reasonably have been hoped. Niebuhr avers that, with a fair degree of consistency, Biblical and Christian thought, at least in the Augustinian tradition, has maintained that "pride" is the essence of sin. (In effect, it is being assumed here that his statement is a fair reflection of the situation in orthodox theology.) And then Niebuhr actually writes: "Our present interest is to relate the Biblical and distinctively Christian conception of sin as pride and self-love to the observable behaviour of men." [72] What more could be desired? For the intention here is precisely the other side of this coin—to relate the observable behavior of a woman to the distinctively Christian conception of sin as pride. There are five elements of the analysis made in Chapter I that will be compared with Niebuhr's account.

1. The first point more strictly is concerned with the background to pride. The analysis of Mrs. Jackson's situation was entered into in terms of "the *tension* inherent in responsible creaturehood." What was in mind here was the apparently contradictory emphases running through the Scriptures, on the one hand inculcating standing on one's own feet, and on the other stressing God's initiative together with advocating becoming like little children. Whatever the correct exegesis of particular verses, there seems to be a place for both autonomy and dependence, both self-development and reliance on others.

The end result envisioned fits well with developmental psychology as I understand it. From the virtually total dependence on others in infancy, a striving toward autonomy increasingly gathers momentum. And only he who achieves an identity separate from his parents, who becomes a self, can enter into mature creative commitments and relationships, be they to work, to marriage, to parenthood, or to God. The normative process seems to move from a predominant dependence through an emphasis on independence to an interdependence that is neither overly dependent nor falsely independent. Failure to move on through this process would obviously afford a potent matrix for pride if development is arrested at the middle state. For one form this could take would be a continuing adolescent attempt unrealistically to maintain an exaggerated independence.

As far as can be determined, this is not essentially dissimilar to the backdrop of pride as Niebuhr describes it. Sin is occasioned, though not caused, by the contradiction between finiteness and freedom in which man stands. "Man is insecure and involved in natural contingency; he seeks to overcome this insecurity by a will-to-power which overreaches the limits of human creatureliness." [73] "Sin is not merely the error of overestimating human capacities. . . . The fact is that man is never unconscious of his weakness, of the limited and dependent character of his existence and knowledge. The occasion for his temptation lies in . . . his greatness and his weakness . . . taken together." [74] "Anxiety is the internal precondition of sin, . . . the internal description of the state of temptation." [75]

With regard to the roots of the deluded human attempt to play God, then, these two descriptions are not antagonistic, although couched in very different terms. The writer's understanding of the developmental *process*, not derived directly from this case, does lead to some differences of emphasis which will be noted at the end of this section.

2. The second point at which it is necessary to turn to Niebuhr is occasioned by a confession of ignorance made in the course of the case analysis. Does the orthodox connotation of "pride" involve grasping at both the power and the perfection of God? The question was raised because the author was struck by the fact that any self-righteousness in Mrs. Jackson appeared to be very subdominant if it was there at all. At this point, Niebuhr's book offers a clear-cut answer. "It will be convenient in this analysis to distinguish between three types

of pride, which are, however, never completely distinct in actual life: pride of power, pride of knowledge and pride of virtue." [76] Moreover, he avers that this is a traditional distinction in Christian thought. Mrs. Jackson, then, does not fall outside his categories. She would do so only if she went about her "divine" chores with a simple modesty and humility and a total absence of self-satisfaction at how indispensable she was.

3. At a third point, too, Niebuhr basically supplies an answer to something that puzzled me when making the theological analysis in Chapter I. This concerns the dynamics behind pride. I had supposed that a fear of loss of control and overt inadequacy typically underlay a need to control. Consequently, it came as a surprise that Mrs. Jackson did not appear markedly angry, afraid, or ashamed, in this crisis that was so clearly marked by her loss of control.

Niebuhr explicitly distinguishes two kinds of dynamics underlying pride of power. "There is a pride of power in which the human ego assumes its self-sufficiency and self-mastery and imagines itself secure against all vicissitudes." [77] His example of this type is the supreme confidence of Great Britain in the heyday of the Empire—a confidence with good reason. In the other situation, dynamically, "the ego does not feel secure and therefore grasps for more power in order to make itself secure. It does not regard itself as sufficiently significant or respected or feared, and therefore seeks to enhance its position in nature and society." [78] These dynamics are typical of the "have-nots" and the underprivileged. In short: "In the one case the ego seems unconscious of the finite and determinate character of its existence. In the other case the lust for power is prompted by a darkly conscious realization of its insecurity." [79]

That much seems so obvious that I feel I ought to have thought of it. Yet though Niebuhr describes two underlying dynamics of pride that are almost opposite to one another he makes no remark concerning what happens when each is shattered. The implication would seem to follow that failure of the first type of pride would come as a genuine surprise of shocked amazement; for the second, as a confirmation of their worst and most repressed fears. It would seem worth pursuing both theological analysis and the implications for ministry at this point. Provisionally, though, Mrs. Jackson would seem to fit better into the former category, although we do not pretend to understand how she came to be like this. However, it should be noted that Niebuhr partially retracts the distinction he has made. For he claims that neither Adler nor Horney fully appreciated how deep the insecurity runs in human nature. Therefore the distinction between the two types is only provisional. Even the strongest monarch or tyrant (and his examples may not be the most suitable choices) "is driven to assert himself beyond measure partly by a sense of insecurity." [80]

4. The fourth point is treated here only as it relates to pride. Substantively it falls in the next section. Moreover, it is not fully apparent from the verbatims in Chapter I, but becomes clearer the more Mrs. Jackson is heard from. In the first conversation, Mrs. Jackson shows some signs of having "reached bottom." She is willing, at least verbally, to acknowledge that she has been arrogating to herself some of the divine prerogatives. (To what extent she really feels this or, further, recognizes it as sin, is another matter.) But as later conversations made plain, the moment Mrs. Jackson began to feel a little better, she was willing to get back on the throne complete with full regalia, orb and scepter. And so it went, back and forth, until it began to seem that she could only acknowledge that she is not God in the presence of immediate and utter chaos. It was precisely this *oscillation* in her pride, or her recognition of her pride, that was a further question raised. (Perhaps the model of the alcoholic is a parallel, for in that case one or more relapses after the initial euphoria of having licked the problem with the help of his new friends is half expected by AA.)

Niebuhr does not address himself to the problem in these

terms. But in treating the element of *deceit* involved in pride, he seems to throw some light on what underlies this oscillation (and again modifies the absoluteness of the dichotomous dynamics he posited in the previous point).

> Our analysis of man's sin of pride and self-love has consistently assumed that an element of deceit is involved in this self-glorification. . . . Man loves himself inordinately. Since his determinate existence does not deserve the devotion lavished upon it, it is obviously necessary to practice some deception in order to justify such excessive devotion. While such deception is constantly directed against competing wills, seeking to secure their acceptance and validation of the self's too generous opinion of itself, its primary purpose is to deceive, not others, but the self.[81]

But this complex deception is neither pure ignorance nor conscious distortion in each instance. "Willing ignorance," Tertullian called it.[82] The sinful self needs its deception because the truth that, finite and determined as it is, it does not deserve unconditional devotion, is never wholly obscured. "The desperate effort to deceive others must, therefore, be regarded as, on the whole, an attempt to aid the self in believing a pretension it cannot easily believe because it was itself the author of the deception."[83] Yet the deceptions are never wholly convincing to the ego. "Yet the deception never becomes so completely a part of the self that it could be regarded as a condition of ignorance. In moments of crisis the true situation may be vividly revealed to the self, prompting it to despairing remorse or possibly to a more creative contrition."[84] Or, as would seem to be the case with Mrs. Jackson, prompting to a temporary recognition of the true situation, which the deceitful self is able to discard the moment the pressure lightens!

5. The final question raised by the theological analysis in Chapter I concerned the (unverifiable) possibility that Mrs.

Jackson's overweening *pride* and playing God to her family had contributed to their own abject surrender and inability to be responsible—or vice versa. What are the possible forms of interplay and varying consequences of arrogation of power by one human being and capitulation by those around him?

At this point, Niebuhr's analysis is deficient. He notes in general that "all human life is involved in the sin of seeking security at the expense of other life." [85] And his discussion of the attempt to deceive others in the service of the deception of the self has just been noted. He also has an extended consideration of forms of *group* pride, such as national or racial pride, and its ramifications.[86] But of the effect of individual pride on those intimately related to the person; or the part played by undue dependency among the members of one's family as increasing the temptation to pride for an individual, he has nothing to say. Yet Brunner's words would appear to be very apropos:

> It is only pure spirits . . . who can sin simply from pure arrogance . . . [in the case of man].
>
> It is a fruit that attracts, it is a whispered doubt which stirs, it is the dream of being like God which turns the scale.[87]

From this I conclude that Mrs. Jackson could not just have decided "out of the blue" to be like God. Some tempting opportunity, such as offered by her family, was a necessary precondition.

Perhaps it is broadly true that Christian thought has hitherto concentrated on either the individual or mankind in its treatment of sin. But if it can lay as much stress on the family with respect to baptism as it undoubtedly does in the Reformed tradition, then further analysis of pride at the interpersonal, as well as at the racial and individual levels can reasonably be called for.

To make any *claims* on the basis of a tentative analysis of one verbatim and a comparison with one theologian would be foolhardy. What is possible, though, is to try to chart where the five points of dialogue between the theological analysis of the case and Niebuhr's systematic exposition fall in terms of the theoretical possibilities outlined in the section on methodology.

At two points, the analysis of the pastoral case would appear to illustrate elements of the traditional Christian understanding of pride, as this is represented by Niebuhr. This is the position with respect to the possibility of pride of power existing with very little accompanying self-righteousness. That one of two alternative underlying dynamics of pride is a hitherto undented self-confidence also fits here. These are contributions to theology on level one in the categories proposed, i.e., concrete illustrations or examples of what Niebuhr describes.

The fourth observation that was discussed is perhaps best classified as a second-level contribution (i.e., of question-raising, corrective value to theology). It may be correct to understand the oscillation in Mrs. Jackson's manifest pride as a reflection of the tension between the pressure of reality and the power of self-deception, where the pressure of reality is itself variable. Niebuhr does not explicitly mention this feature of oscillation. Yet the phenomenon was sufficiently marked in Mrs. Jackson's case to justify asking how common it is. And if it is widespread, Niebuhr's description at this point might well be enlarged to include it.

The first and the fifth points of our analysis, however, may at least point to possible contributions at the third level, i.e., as constructive supplements to traditional orthodoxy. The first issue concerned the background to sin. The basic understanding of the possibility of sin residing in the tension between man's finitude and freedom was not disputed. But a serious question was raised concerning the part played by necessary developmental processes. If these in any way suggest the inevitability of this potential for sin being actualized—in the course of the appropriate establishment of a sense of identity and selfhood—they constitute a very significant consideration. The final issue concerned the middle-range, interpersonal workings of human sinfulness. For the *interaction* of members of the Jackson family was clearly a highly charged dynamic factor. As such, it merits careful consideration; but Niebuhr passes over interaction at this level in silence.

While it is not the purpose of this essay to furnish outside support for the theological suggestions raised by the case material, I cannot resist citing two authors whom I have just read. Peter Homans commends the potential contribution of psychoanalytic psychology to theology because it speaks to the issues that confront the developing self. In contrast, he points out, "Niebuhr's anthropological analyses require a fully developed self." [88] Furthermore, he explicitly criticizes Niebuhr because "there is no sustained analysis of family dynamics. . . . Niebuhr's innocent family is rationalized and sentimental, a betrayal of his own Biblical realism." [89] Bernard Loomer similarly speaks to both of these issues. While concurring with Niebuhr that most modern accounts of the self lack an adequate understanding of man in his self-transcendence, he goes on to say: "But I also think that Niebuhr, like most theologians, lacks a basically social conception of the self." [90] He sees this as equally important. "The theory of the social nature of the self means more than the idea that the individual is fulfilled through his participation in the lives of others (Tillich). It means that the self is constituted by others, that the self is an emergent from its relations, whether this is understood in the manner of Mead or Whitehead. The unity of the self is an achievement, not a presupposition." [91]

In one sense, citing these references "demotes" the contributions of the case material to level one. They become concrete illustrations for one theological position over against another, although in relation to Niebuhr they still operate at level three. But in any case there are no pretentious claims to uniqueness being made for the insights from the pastoral situation. Their value lies in their documented facticity.

## HOPE

For more than one reason, this section will not be as clear-cut a point-by-point comparison of the phenomenological situation and Christian theology as the previous one. To begin with, the data are more diffuse. There does not appear to be such an unequivocal description of a particular issue for theology, although it is being gathered together under the rubric of "hope." Indeed, this in itself compounds the problem. For whereas, theologically, "pride" describes sinful man, and its relevance was easy to see, in Christian terminology "hope" has always been a virtue.[92] And all too often there is little point of contact between Mrs. Jackson's hopes and what Christian doctrine is talking about.

The lack of a single theological source giving adequate consideration to the whole range of human hoping and the relation of Christian hope to this is a major drawback. Jürgen Moltmann will be the principal theologian treated. And he does claim that the doctrine of Christian hope embraces both the object hoped for and also the hope inspired by it.[93] He even asserts that the Christian hope cannot be considered "distinct from the minor hopes that are directed towards visible changes in human life, neither can it as a result dissociate itself from such hopes by relegating them to a different sphere while considering its own future to be supraworldly and purely spiritual in character." [94] Nevertheless, it will become clear that Moltmann's treatment of hoping is too limited in scope to shed light on all the issues raised by the concrete human situation.[95]

Pastoral theology in the strict sense would be limited to a dialogue between the reflections on the case and Moltmann's exposition. But this would be largely a non-conversation, more reminiscent of Kipling's "The Ballad of East and West" where "never the twain shall meet" than anything else. But the immediate pastoral relevance in the life of the church is too pressing for this to be justifiable. It is repeatedly a question of whether, to put it bluntly, a person's hopes deserve to be encouraged or should have cold water poured on them. Accordingly a number of other witnesses—philosophers, psychiatrists, and psychologists—will also be heard.[96]

A brief recapitulation of Mrs. Jackson's situation is in order here. From the outside, the turmoil looks pretty overwhelming. Her husband's physical and emotional health are at a low ebb, and for some time he has been unable to function as a father-provider, even at a level that would be adequate although lower than that to which they have been accustomed. Mrs. Jackson's own physical and emotional state is now no better than her husband's. In consequence she is able neither to contribute an independent income as has been the case until recently, nor to boss (ramrod) the family and maintain its stability (at whatever cost) thereby. The two elder daughters have both shown evidence of moderate to severe dysfunction. And now the family is dispersed, practically to the four winds.

1. Mrs. Jackson's response to this chaotic situation at first glance seems to amount to "despair." Not only has everything collapsed at once, but every time she gets back on her feet and attempts to organize a general recovery, no one else helps in emergency measures and she falls on her face again. She cannot see a toehold by which she can begin to climb out of the pit. Yet the question we were left with was: Can this be called true despair? For though she can see the pit and also that there is no obvious escape route, she is still looking for one. She has not accepted the strong likelihood that she will spend the rest of her life with things much as they are, that there may be *no* exit, at least within her present frame of reference, no "healing" in the sense of a restoration of even part of the previous state of affairs. In short, Mrs. Jackson hasn't "given up." [97]

Moltmann's discussion of despair, in the context of the specifically Christian hope, does not bear on Mrs. Jackson's situation directly but does reveal his understanding of some of the dynamics of both despair and hope. "Despair is the premature, arbitrary anticipation of the non-fulfillment of what we hope for from God." [98] But he claims that despair presupposes hope, quoting Augustine to the effect that what we do not long for can be the object neither of our hope nor of our despair. This is unexceptionable. But he continues: "The pain of despair surely lies in the fact that a hope is there, but no way opens up towards its fulfillment. . . . Hence despair would seek to preserve the soul from disappointments." [99] To equate hope with a wish or longing, and to speak of "hope" when there is no expectation, no possibility envisaged, contradicts the commonsense meaning of the term and does not seem helpful. [100]

2. The second element that was puzzling was the range of Mrs. Jackson's attitudes (not so much her mood, which was rather flat throughout) about essentially the same set of circumstances. It would seem more common for a person to feel happy about a situation he perceives as desirable, depressed about one he regards as bad, and more or less neutral about anything in between. But with Mrs. Jackson it is not so, at least insofar as her words can even be taken at anything near face value. She feels something akin to despair at times, at other times is ambivalent, and at yet other times is strikingly optimistic—about essentially the same total situation. The most minimal change in her external circumstances—not having a headache, or having had a day's rest in bed—is enough to renew all her hopeful feelings and have her lightly discount all the sobering and negative elements in the outlook.

The point here concerns *the grounds* of hope. This will have to be pursued later from another angle. Suffice it to say that there is nothing evident to the outside observer to suggest adequate external grounds for Mrs. Jackson's expectation that "all in the garden will be lovely" in the way it used to be. Clearly her hopes are otherwise grounded than the specifically

Christian hope, the guaranteed external basis for which is Jesus Christ and his future as the Risen One. There are no indications whatsoever that Mrs. Jackson's hopes ultimately rest on this. But Moltmann holds that "the question whether all statements about the future are grounded in the person and history of Jesus Christ provides it (Christian eschatology) with the touchstone by which to distinguish Christian hopes from utopias." [101]

3. The previous statement by Moltmann has led on to the issue of *the content* of a person's hopes. For in Christian doctrine the grounds and the content of hope are closely related; both are defined by reference to the risen Christ. "Hope is nothing else than the expectation of those things which faith has believed to have been truly promised by God." [102] As is well known, Moltmann's emphasis is not on the traditional "hereafter" but on the historic future. Hope is "a passion for what has been made possible" by God. So hopeful faith becomes an impatience with reality as it is, a protest at and contradiction of it. However, this would seem to make it even more incumbent upon him to explicate both the distinctions between and the relations between Christian hoping and other human hoping.

In one respect, Moltmann's description of the Christian hope is compatible with Marcel's analysis. For the latter has stressed that hope is different from wishing, daydreaming, or deluding oneself, in the sense that it has only a *global* object. His dictum that hope "tends inevitably to transcend the particular objects to which it is attached" [103] finds support from an eminent psychiatrist:

> Wishes and dreams have specific objects and articulate contents; hoping is vaguer and more diffuse. There is a difference between "I hope" and "I hope that . . ." The more specific the "that" the more likely that a wish, an illusion or a delusion is at hand. What a person can truly hope for is very broad and global, such as deliverance, liberation, life.[104]

On the other hand, Stotland's whole explication of hope is quite different. His definition of hope as an expectation greater than zero of achieving a goal has already been noted. Consequent upon this is one of his major hypotheses: "The greater the expectation of attaining a goal, the more likely the individual will act to attain it." [105] This simply cannot be positively related to the traditional statement of the Christian hope, according to which the individual neither has to nor can engage in overt "action" to attain it. But it would seem that when the emphasis is on the historic future, as with Moltmann, "the hope" and Christian life and action may be more directly related.

Be that as it may, it is evident that Mrs. Jackson's hopes were quite specific. When she spoke globally of the future bringing things, she was quite clearly envisioning a restoration of the state her family had heretofore enjoyed. Her preoccupation with maintaining the standards to which she was accustomed, at least as she focused the immediate problem, came across very forcibly—so much so that it seemed she might go on "hoping against hope" if her wishes were not fulfilled. Yet this is not the presumption of which Moltmann writes. "Presumption is a premature, self-willed anticipation of the fulfillment of what we hope for from God." [106] It must be now or never!—and "never" is the opposite sin, despair. But, rather than being willful insistence on the immediate receipt of what God has promised, Mrs. Jackson's focus is on those minor hopes that are directed toward attainable goals and visible changes in human life to which Moltmann has already referred, while only averring that the two kinds of hopes cannot be dissociated. This will be reverted to in a moment.

4. In substantial agreement with Marcel, Pruyser elucidates three closely related aspects of the psychodynamic quality of hoping as he understands it. Especially in view of the deficient delineation at this point in Moltmann, it is worthwhile to consider these.

a. In the first place, he emphasizes that in hoping, the ego does not feel itself as central with respect either to action or feelings (a state of affairs diametrically opposed to willing, and to both doubt and certainty). The attitude of the hoping person

> is one of modesty and humility before the nature of reality. The chastity and humility of hoping can be seen from the relation between hoping and its global object. Hoping is not predicting that such and such must happen. It is entirely outside the sphere of rights and certainties. . . . Phenomenologically, hoping is connected with patience and forbearance. Hoping involves waiting, though with an added quality of awaiting. Wishing, on the contrary, is clearly associated with urges toward tension discharge.[107]

Mrs. Jackson's hoping does not appear to fit well at all with this definition. (It may be that "pride" is intrinsically inimical to hope defined in this way.) Mrs. Jackson herself, or the extension of herself in her family, is central to her feelings and in her expectations of achieving the outcome for which she looks. However, it would seem that Moltmann's emphasis on action with respect to the open future would also make the ego more central in the Christian hope as thus redefined, without of course making it primary.

b. Furthermore, Pruyser is careful to note that it must be recognized that in the last resort reality is always subjectively perceived. His point is that it is somewhat presumptuous to judge another man's attitude toward reality as being so erroneous that his hopes are unjustified, because the boundaries of reality are fluid and uncertain.

Even granting this, surely it is true that "wishing for the moon" may need to be discouraged. But it does bring us to the question, against which we have already brushed, of the relation of Mrs. Jackson's hopes to "reality." As was remarked, her appraisal struck me as totally unrealistic, and irritated me accordingly. From what I knew of the attitude of concerned

third parties, there was no possibility of some of her hopes,
such as of regaining her job, being fulfilled—and that her
artistic illusions would be realized seemed even more improbable. All this is simply to say that Mrs. Jackson's perception
of possibilities was very different from that of the outside observer. But because her hoping was based almost entirely on
internal subjective probabilities, rather than external conditions, it was particularly difficult to assess.

Moltmann is less than helpful here. In appraising hope as
over against either presumption or despair, he writes:

> Hope alone is to be called "realistic," because it alone
> takes seriously the possibilities with which all reality
> is fraught. . . . Earthly hopes . . . anticipate what is
> possible to reality, historic and moving as it is, and
> use their influence to decide the processes of history.
> Thus hopes and anticipations . . . are realistic ways
> of perceiving the scope of our real possibilities . . .
> for they do not strive after things which have "no
> place," but after things that have "no place as yet"
> but can acquire one.[108]

The criterion of "real" possibilities is evidently being in line
with God's purposes. But this is exceedingly difficult to apply
accurately, in discriminating between the *welter* of short-term
real possibilities. For here we only see "through a glass
darkly."

c. The third aspect of the psychodynamic quality of hoping
concerns the degree of conviction that is implied, and is most
important for our general consideration. Marcel and Pruyser
are agreed that hoping can arise only out of calamity and
despair—and indeed, that this "un-hope" or despair remains
dynamically active as a background.

> If reality does not first give us reasons for despairing,
> it cannot give us grounds for hoping. . . . and indeed,
> since despairing is a form of appraising reality in re-

lation to ourselves, its continued activity in hoping is one safeguard against falling into illusions and other forms of reality distortion. For hoping is not denial of reality, but a continued reevaluation of its content in contrast to other possible evaluations.[109]

Pruyser makes the further distinction that despair is always a narcissistic state, whereas hoping is not. Fear, doubt, and despair accentuate one's sense of self-importance. Hoping is an urge toward deliverance, "not only from 'the situation' (the external conditions) but also from a too much loved self (the internal conditions)." [110]

If this be so, that true hope can arise only out of genuine despair like phoenix from the ashes, there is no hope for Mrs. Jackson until she loses hope, paradoxical as that sounds.

5. In my previous article on the subject, I suggested that there seem to be three main criteria in terms of which human hope can be evaluated—its contribution to sustaining life, the merit of its object or content, and the dynamic intrapsychic processes involved. It was the thesis of that article that all three of these interrelated criteria have to be taken into account; that no single one of them is an adequate basis for evaluating a person's hope by itself.[111]

Of those criteria, that of survival value has hardly been applied to Mrs. Jackson's hoping. Moltmann's basic comment with respect to the Christian hope is that "neither in presumption nor in despair does there lie the power to renew life, but only in hope that is enduring and sure." [112] This, of course, is viewing the matter from the long-term perspective—but this is not the only one.

There is insufficient evidence (as usual) to determine the precise part played by Mrs. Jackson's hopes in her survival. But it does not seem unreasonable to suppose that others in like situations but without her hopes might well take their own life, literally or symbolically. Unrealistic or not, it is difficult not to admire the sheer guts of this woman's hoping.

At the same time, granting a causal connection between her hopes and survival at her present level, it must be wondered whether her hopes do not actually impede improvement of that situation. Recalling the function of the hopes of the American slaves in enabling them to survive in slavery, but perhaps at the expense of inclining them to put up with slavery, it was noted in the article referred to that "there are situations in which survival is not the most desirable value, but change, and that hopes that are too future-oriented and compensatory may impede such change." [113] In this case, it would seem to be hopes that are too past-oriented that may be impeding necessary reorientation as a prelude to improvement. It is precisely the narrow vision of a return of the "status quo ante crisis" that hinders.

It is not family disintegration, per se, or having to be a cleaning woman to keep body and soul together, that would be the improvement, of course. (Mrs. Jackson would protest volubly against any such appraisal of reality!) The potential improvement would lie in cause for despair such that she could no longer place her hopes in her own goals and actions and might, just might, become open to the good things God has in store for her. This is to say that while her hopes may be sustaining her life as it is, it is precisely this life which she has to lose if she is to save it! But even there, insofar as "while there's life there's hope," her present hopes are serving to maintain the life that may one day become open to God and his purposes. And the snag for all practical purposes is that there is no guarantee that the loss of her short-term earthly hopes will be accompanied by a moving *through* despair to a truly Christian hope, even though this becomes potentially a greater possibility as her false hopes founder one by one.

This dialogue between Mrs. Jackson's human hoping and the Christian hope as explicated by Moltmann has been very difficult to carry through. Nor is this simply a result of a poor choice of principal witnesses. For Stotland's broad investigation of human hoping is couched in terms that do not easily

leave room for the Christian hope. And while Marcel and
Pruyser describe a phenomenology and dynamics of hoping
that accord well with the latter, they rule out much that
would naturally be called "hoping." It just does not seem possible to dismiss what Moltmann calls "the minor hopes that are
directed towards attainable goals and visible changes in human life" along with wishes and illusions. It was noted that in
one or two ways, Moltmann's rephrasing of the Christian hope
lends itself slightly more to some of Stotland's analysis than
did the traditional doctrine. Nevertheless, there is a great distinction drawn here, one that is insupportable from the standpoint of common sense. Whatever the subtle differences of
quality, in essence the great human hopes and the everyday
ones are too similar to justify calling one "hope" and the other
something else.

In short, there is apparent an urgent need for a more inclusive Christian anthropology at the point of hoping, that
explicates the relation as well as the obvious differences between the one great hope and all the others. At the simplest
level, for instance, what ordinary human hoping is legitimate
for one who holds his ultimate hope in Christ?

## DEPENDENCE

The reflections on Mr. Jackson's situation in Chapter III
revolved around the subject of dependence. It will be remem-
bered that there were numerous indications of his long-term
reliance both on other people and on alcohol and drugs during
the course of his adult life. At the same time it was also known
—and very significant to Mr. Jackson himself—that he had
been able, given these supports, to function as a father-provider for some twenty years. But a major upheaval, in the form
of sudden unemployment through no fault of his own, proved
too much for him to cope with successfully. Thereupon a vi-
cious downward spiral in the whole family situation set in.

The theological sources with which comparisons and con-
trasts will be drawn in this connection are somewhat diverse.
Schleiermacher's concept of dependence and Tillich's of "participation" are so closely integrated with the respective authors' total systems that, like spaghetti, they really need to be
taken up as a whole. Yet because these are such important
authorities, an attempt will be made to relate what they have
to say to Mr. Jackson's situation at several places. The dialogue with Reinhold Niebuhr will also be resumed at one
point. There are four closely related aspects of dependence
to be considered.

1. The first question concerns the *quantity* of *appropriate*
dependence on other human beings. For to acknowledge interdependence as both proper and inescapable says nothing
about the proportion of dependence that is legitimate therein.
It has been suggested that Mrs. Jackson's overt dominance in
the family almost certainly met some of Mr. Jackson's needs
as well as some of her own. The significant fact is that, until
the last two years, the family was able to cohere and function
on the basis of this arrangement. So apart from cultural preju-
dices, what was wrong with it? The implosion that has taken
place is no more evidence that it was inherently unstable than
is the difficulty for the average widow of taking over her late
husband's business affairs. This raises the question of whether
we should not think of "appropriate dependence" on others in
terms of a *varying* level that is suited to the particular personalities involved. For it is by no means clear that quantity is a
sufficient criterion of appropriateness, even though terms such
as "overdependence" have a primarily quantitative connotation. Of the theologians looked at, Schleiermacher comes clos-
est to addressing himself to this issue. He describes our relations to nature, including other human beings, as a *reciprocity*
made up of on the one hand a dependence or receptivity and
on the other a freedom or activity.[114] He maintains that neither
dependence nor freedom will ever disappear completely. But
he observes that whereas the feeling of dependence predom-

inates in the relation of children to their parents, this gradu-
ally diminishes.[115]

No one is likely to dispute that a child, or someone who is
mentally defective, is quite properly more dependent than
adults. But can such distinctions not be extended to adults
with personalities having varying strengths and limitations?
Where this might become important is in a fuller consideration of its influence on a man's ability to depend on God, and
the quality and extent of that dependence.

To turn attention to the quality of appropriate dependence
is to change the crucial pastoral question from "How dependent is he?" to "How is he dependent?"

2. For even supposing that the appropriate level of dependence on other human beings is relative rather than fixed, this
does not give Mrs. Jackson *carte blanche*. Yet it was noted that
when in the event of total family breakdown a "committee of
five" stepped in, on at least one significant level Mr. Jackson
was perfectly willing for them simply to "take over." Whatever his quibbles with regard to the way they went about it,
he recognized his immediate need of support—and was willing to take it where he could get it.

At this point alarm bells begin to ring in my mind, and I
wondered if Mr. Jackson was not *too* ready and willing to be
taken care of. Was his long-term pattern of mobilizing one
support base after another fully justified by personal limitations with which he had come to terms? Or was there an element there, not solely of not being up to coping with all the
demands and strains of life, but also of having found satisfactions that more than compensated for the incapacity? Is there
revealed, in other words, not merely an inadequate or crippled
self, but a too quick contentment with this to the point of using it to justify failing even to be the best self he could be?

It is instructive at this point to resume the dialogue with
Reinhold Niebuhr. According to his analysis, unlike animals
man "seeks to protect himself against nature's contingencies;
but he cannot do so without transgressing the limits which

have been set for his life. Therefore all human life is involved
in the sin of seeking security at the expense of other life." [116]
But while this is partly descriptive of Mr. Jackson, it does not
seem to fit him entirely. He is involved in the "sin of seeking
security at the expense of other life" to the extent that he "uses"
other people for his security blanket. For his emotional-black-
mail techniques may be not one whit less coercive and controlling than Mrs. Jackson's dominant management style. On
the other hand, he is anything but "transgressing the limits
which have been set for his life" in the sense of trying to be
like God, which is how Niebuhr means it.

Nor does his life-style fit into Niebuhr's other major category of sin: sensuality. For by this, Niebuhr means "any inordinate devotion to a mutable good." [117] The forms of sensuality he considers are gluttony, drunkenness, luxurious and
extravagant living, and sexual license. And he states that, in
contrast to "the destruction of life's harmony by the self's attempt to centre life around itself, sensuality would seem to be
the destruction of harmony within the self, by the self's undue
identification with the devotion to particular impulses and de-
sires within itself." [118]

Instead, with Mr. Jackson, there seems to be a failure to as-
pire to the possibilities of human life, a settling too easily for
too little rather than a grasping after too much. Yet this is
different again from the kind of failure to be a self which
Valerie Goldstein describes. Her critique of "male" theology is
explicitly directed at its "most uncompromising expression"
in the writings of Anders Nygren and Reinhold Niebuhr,
which delineates sin as the self's attempt to overcome anxiety
by magnifying its own power, righteousness, or knowledge,
and commends self-giving love as the very opposite. And she
makes a strong case for the "feminine" version of sin being
"better suggested by such items as . . . lack of an organizing
center or focus, . . . in short, underdevelopment or negation
of self" as a consequence of *too much* self-giving.[119] In contrast to this, while Mr. Jackson may well have an underdevel-

oped self, there is nothing to indicate that this is a consequence of his having poured himself out for others.

Here we may have isolated another phenomenological manifestation of sin that Niebuhr misses, in addition to the one
described by Goldstein. Moreover, my hunch would be that it
is a rather common variety, and not a mere anomaly that falls
between the cracks of the two main forms, be these pride and
sensuality or "masculine" and "feminine." It is characterized
by an "inordinate devotion to a mutable good"—but that good
is the self. It does not transgress the limits that have been
set for life. It does not lose its center because it spends itself
on others. Rather, it is a careful selfishness that nicely calcu-
lates "how far it can go" in using others for its own security.
And the end result of this full-time maintenance operation of
the self is worse than the result of the miser's hoarding. Radical depreciation sets in, and one is left hugging a dried,
wrinkled prune!

3. The third issue that concerns another aspect of the *quality* of appropriate dependence was raised in Chapter III in
terms of the relation between dependence and trust. For it
did seem that the nature of Mr. Jackson's attachment to his
various means of support, human as well as nonhuman, was
esentially functional. Rather than any personal investment in
and commitment to them, it seemed to be a relationship based
solely on use. Thus when any given support failed to fulfill its
function, detachment from it was no great problem, and cast-
ing around for a replacement was the main concern. This may
or may not be fair to Mr. Jackson. His apparent lack of concern for his wife, for example, may be largely a manifestation
of medically induced tranquillity, and a purely temporary
phenomenon.

Nevertheless, this does raise the issue of what may be a
subtle distinction between dependence and something else.
I have always thought of dependence, as in the case of an
alcoholic and his bottle, as being an attachment so deep that
withdrawal was traumatic. But may it be that there is a vari-

ety of "dependence" that is able to substitute any given object
or person for another without pain, inasmuch as the form of
the support is irrelevant so long as it functions adequately?
This would seem to go hand in hand with an awareness of
the sources of gratification only as-they-relate-to-oneself, and
not as-they-are-in-themselves.

At this point we turn to Tillich's analyses of individualiza-
tion and participation and their strict interdependence. Mr.
Jackson's relations with people go beyond that which Tillich
calls "non-personal encounters," using walking in a crowd or
reading about people in the newspaper as examples.[120] But
they are a far cry from "communion," "participation in another
completely centred and completely individual self." [121] If our
analysis is accurate, it is less even than the "ambiguity of personal participation." "In every act of participation there is an
element of holding one's self back and an element of giving
one's self. In the attempts to know the other one, self-seclu-
sion expresses itself in the projection of images of the other's
being which disguise his real being and are only projections of
the one who attempts to know." [122] For this presumes that
there is an element of self-giving and an attempt, at least, to
know the other one.

Tillich's position, of course, is that "in the state of estrangement man is shut within himself and cut off from participation." [123] But the issue here is the form this takes. Later Tillich
is a little more explicit about the forms of estrangement or
bondage:

> Disintegration means failure to reach or to preserve
> self-integration. This failure can occur in one of two
> directions. Either it is the inability to overcome a
> limited, stabilized, and immovable centeredness, in
> which case there is a center, but a center which does
> not have a life process whose content is changed and
> increased; thus it approaches the death of mere self-
> identity. Or it is the inability to return because of the
> dispersing power of the manifoldness, in which case

there is life, but it is dispersed and weak in centered-
ness, and it faces the danger of losing its center altogether—the death of mere self-alteration.[124]

4. The final problem concerns the relation between dependence on human others and dependence on God. What is the
nature and extent of the continuities and/or discontinuities involved? Are these identical processes in terms of their dynamics, and merely distinguished according to the object-person?
Can mature dependence on God, like creative interdependence in marriage, only follow on the establishment of a measure of genuine identity and autonomy?

Schleiermacher addresses these issues in explicating religion
as "the feeling of absolute dependence." As one commentator
writes regarding that definition:

> *Absolute* stands for the fact that the relationship to
> God is perceptible as an ingredient of self-conscious-
> ness only because it exists along with other relation-
> ships from which it distinguishes itself in kind. That
> is to say, the absolute relationship presupposes, in the
> order of awareness, relative relationships; . . .[125]

Moreover, "absolute dependence does not . . . supersede relative dependence." [126]

Schleiermacher actually posits "three grades of self-consciousness"—the confused animal grade, the sensible self-consciousness, and the feeling of absolute dependence. With respect to the continuity and discontinuity between them, he
says:

> While the lowest or animal grade of consciousness
> gradually disappears as the middle grade develops,
> the highest cannot develop at all so long as the lowest
> is present; but, on the other hand, the middle grade
> must persist undiminished even when the highest has
> reached its perfect development. . . . It is impossible
> to claim a constancy for the highest self-consciousness,

except on the supposition that the sensible self-consciousness is always conjoined with it. Of course, this
conjunction cannot be regarded as a fusion of the
two. . . . It means rather a co-existence of the two
in the same moment. . . .[127]

Are remnants of the lowest grade of consciousness still lin-
gering in Mr. Jackson, thus ruling out the very possibility of
the highest? And is this the same as saying that he hasn't
achieved a sufficient sense of identity? Whether or not these
be the facts of the case, it does seem that the highest level of
self-consciousness, the feeling of absolute dependence or of
the irreducible givenness of the self, is missing in Mr. Jackson.
Does this, then, inevitably imply that he misappropriates all
relative dependencies? Schleiermacher does not say, but such
a conclusion would be compatible with the general Christian
understanding of sin or estrangement.

If the situation were different, it might be important to go
a step farther and ask whether absolute dependence on God
contributes to a greater independence of human others.
Schleiermacher seems to imply this when he states that the
higher comes to predominate "so that in the immediate self-
consciousness the sensible determination asserts itself rather
as an opportunity for the appearance of the feeling of absolute dependence" whatever the outward circumstances.[128] But
the question of temporal priority with respect to a sense of
identity and a right relationship with God is uncomfortably
akin to the old riddle: Which came first, the chicken or the
egg? And in any case, by the time one looks at a concrete human situation, they are thoroughly scrambled together!

Only on the basis of at least provisional answers to some of
these hard theoretical issues can there be clear grounds for an
authoritative ministry to Mr. Jackson. The concern is how best
to help him escape from the "salvation" that has become a
bondage to him. For presumably he developed his mode of life
as a solution to some strong needs. As Christians, we may be-

lieve there is a better solution. Yet it is obviously not a simple
task to enable him to transfer his allegiance from one support
base to another.

We can only attempt to prepare the way, leaving the final
step to God's grace. Nevertheless, consideration both of the
best way and of what the final situation might look like are
in order. Some of the issues previously discussed are relevant
here. For instance, is there anything in the idea that it would
be easier for a person who invests emotionally in the human
beings on whom he depends, to move toward an appropriate
dependence on God? If so, ways might have to be sought to
facilitate Mr. Jackson risking such an investment of himself in
others. Or again, in thinking of God's providence, of his looking ahead to our true needs, what sort of things can we reasonably expect him to provide? This is a pressing question for
one such as Mr. Jackson, who wants more propping up and
clear-cut instructions than he is ever likely to receive from
God. If the dependency needs of some people are greater than
"average," will God provide more? Or does he expect them to
forage for themselves, and others to minister to them? If the
latter, how can this be done without contributing to the problem as much as to the solution? Again, Schleiermacher defines
the sense of absolute dependence primarily in terms of creatureliness, the awareness of one's life as given. To what extent
should this be accompanied by an attitude of "waiting on the
Lord," implying strictly limited initiative on one's own part?

No neat summing up of the contribution of the case to systematic theological statements of dependence can be made.
This section has raised innumerable questions, rather than
pointed to any clear answers. Yet even more than the previous
sections, it may reinforce the general contention that the
endeavors are worthwhile. For it is the very particularity of
the questions—a particularity and concreteness with which
the minister is forced to grapple every day—that finds the
"systems" not sufficiently precise to be helpful.

# NOTES

1. Seward Hiltner, *Preface to Pastoral Theology* (Abingdon Press, 1958), pp. 20–29.

2. William B. Oglesby, Jr. (ed.), *The New Shape of Pastoral Theology: Essays in Honor of Seward Hiltner* (Abingdon Press, 1969), pp. 40, 164 f.

3. Edward E. Thornton, *Theology and Pastoral Counseling* (Prentice-Hall, Inc., 1964).

4. *Ibid.*, pp. 16–26.

5. Oglesby (ed.), *op. cit.*, p. 148.

6. F. Fiedler, "A Comparison of Therapeutic Relationships in Psychoanalytic, Nondirective and Adlerian Therapy," *J. Consult. Psychol.*, 14 (1950).

7. Part of the discussion of this can be found in: Ian F. McIntosh, "Seeking Forgiveness," *Pastoral Psychology*, Oct. 1971, pp. 51 –56.

8. The English word "pride" is retained despite Tillich's insistence that it cannot adequately render *hubris*, the self-elevation of man into the sphere of the divine. Paul Tillich, *Systematic Theology* (London: James Nisbet & Co., Ltd., 1957), Vol. II, p. 57. No matter which term was chosen, it would be necessary to clarify the sense in which it is being used; and both readability and the comparisons to be made in Chapter V favor the decision made.

9. Cf. William Klassen, *The Forgiving Community* (The Westminster Press, 1966), pp. 119, 163, and James G. Emerson, Jr., *The Dynamics of Forgiveness* (The Westminster Press, 1964), p. 21.

10. Cf. Thornton, *op. cit.*, pp. 85 ff.

11. Willard Gaylin (ed.), *The Meaning of Despair: Psychoanalytic Contributions to the Understanding of Depression* (Science House, Inc., 1968), pp. 388–391.

12. "It seems fair to presume that about 5% of women who become pregnant will have some sort of emotional disturbance following the birth of one of their children." C. L. Kline, "Emotional Illnesses Associated with Childbirth," *American Journal of Obstetrics,* Vol. LXIX (1955), pp. 748–757.

13. Carl R. Rogers, *Client-centered Therapy* (Houghton Mifflin Company, 1951), p. 41.

14. Cf. Don S. Browning, *Atonement and Psychotherapy* (The Westminster Press, 1966), and Thomas C. Oden, *Kerygma and Counseling: Toward a Covenant Ontology for Secular Psychotherapy* (The Westminster Press, 1966).

15. Valerie S. Goldstein, "The Human Situation: A Feminine Viewpoint," *Pastoral Psychology,* April, 1966, pp. 29–42.

16. Thornton, *op. cit.*

17. Gordon W. Allport, *The Person in Psychology* (Beacon Press, Inc., 1968), pp. 81–102. Cf. pp. 88 f.

18. Russell J. Becker, *Family Pastoral Care* (Prentice-Hall, Inc., 1965).

19. Cf. the introductory essay by Daniel Lerner in *Evidence and Inference: The Hayden Colloquium on Scientific Concept and Method,* ed. by Daniel Lerner (The Free Press of Glencoe, 1958).

20. "The commonalities in personality are the horizontal dimensions that run through all individuals. We focus our attention chiefly upon these commonalities; for example, upon the common traits of achievement, anxiety, extraversion, dominance, creativity, or upon the common processes of learning, repression, identification, aging. We spend scarcely one per-

cent of our research time discovering whether these common dimensions are in reality relevant to Bill's personality, and if so how they are patterned together to compose the Billian quality of Bill. Ideally research should explore both horizontal and vertical dimensions." Allport, *The Person in Psychology,* p. 87.

21. Gordon W. Allport, *Letters from Jenny* (Harcourt, Brace & World, Inc., 1965), p. 159.

22. Hiltner and Colston do briefly discuss another kind of shift of relationship—that from a pastoral care relationship to one of counseling, or back again—although this is not one of the dimensions of the context of pastoral counseling on which their data shed specific light. Cf. Seward Hiltner and Lowell G. Colston, *The Context of Pastoral Counseling* (Abingdon Press, 1961), esp. pp. 29–40.

23. Wayne E. Oates, "Making the Contact: Informal Pastoral Relationships," Wayne E. Oates (ed.), *Introduction to Pastoral Counseling* (Broadman Press, 1959), pp. 69–80.

24. Cf. James D. Glasse, *Profession: Minister* (Abingdon Press, 1968), pp. 48–50. Experience suggests that the issues and relationships are more fluid, less clear-cut, than this discussion would suggest.

25. Henry L. Lennard and Arnold Bernstein, "Expectations and Behavior in Therapy," in Bruce J. Biddle and Edwin J. Thomas (eds.), *Role Theory: Concepts and Research* (John Wiley & Sons, Inc., 1966), pp. 179–185.

26. Hiltner, *op. cit.,* pp. 18–20 and 55–69.

27. For a discussion of the pastoral role as coordinator of a much greater number of helping persons and agencies in a different kind of case situation, cf. A. J. van den Blink, "The Minister as Organizer of Caring Services in the Community," *The Journal of Pastoral Care,* June, 1970, pp. 98–108.

28. Bernard Steinzor, *The Healing Partnership* (Harper & Row, Publishers, Inc., 1967), pp. 35 ff.

29. Cf. Ian F. McIntosh, "Contemporary Ministry in a General Hospital," *Pastoral Psychology,* Dec. 1966, pp. 35 ff., for a

discussion of another form in which this question arises.

30. Rogers, *Client-centered Therapy,* and other works.

31. Howard J. Clinebell, Jr., *Basic Types of Pastoral Counseling* (Abingdon Press, 1966).

32. Rogers himself must bear some of the responsibility for this. In his early book, he clearly states his conviction that competent "non-directive" counseling is quicker, venturing as a crude approximation that between six and fifteen contacts should be sufficient. Carl R. Rogers, *Counseling and Psychotherapy: Newer Concepts in Practice* (Houghton Mifflin Company, 1942), p. 232.

33. Cf. Carl R. Rogers and Rosalind F. Dymond (eds.), *Psychotherapy and Personality Change* (The University of Chicago Press, 1954), pp. 259 ff.; Carl R. Rogers (ed.), *The Therapeutic Relationship and Its Impact: A Study of Psychotherapy with Schizophrenics* (The University of Wisconsin Press, 1967), pp. 401 ff.; and Charles B. Truax, "Reinforcement and Nonreinforcement in Rogerian Psychotherapy," *Journal of Abnormal Psychology,* 71 (1966), pp. 1–9.

34. Truax, *loc. cit.*

35. Donald J. Kiesler, Philippa L. Mathieu, and Marjorie H. Klein, "Measurement of Conditions and Process Variables," Ch. 8 in Rogers (ed.), *The Therapeutic Relationship and Its Impact.* It should be noted that their research, which was extensive, careful, and technical, relates to therapy with an exceptional type of clientele. Stated briefly, they found that the level of accurate empathy offered did not become really stable until the eleventh counseling session, and that congruence ratings were considerably less stable over the whole fifteen interviews. Moreover, there was no consistent pattern of relationship between the three therapeutic conditions themselves. *Ibid.,* pp. 157–166.

36. This is not necessarily an argument supporting eclecticism. The eclectic would have to argue that it is some clients or situations that make, for example, Rogerian therapy impossible for *anyone.* If the problem is that no counselor can be consist-

ently Rogerian, the eclectic attempting a client-centered approach is in the same bind as anyone else.

37. Rogers (ed.), *The Therapeutic Relationship and Its Impact*, p. 181.

38. Truax, *loc. cit.*, p. 2.

39. Julian Meltzoff and Melvin Kornreich, *Research in Psychotherapy* (Atherton Press, 1970). A summary of the "outcome" research can be found on pp. 174 ff. The quotation is from p. 220.

40. Clinebell, *op. cit.*

41. *Ibid.*, p. 21.

42. *Ibid.*, p. 67.

43. *Ibid.*, p. 144.

44. *Ibid.*, pp. 144–147.

45. Ian F. McIntosh, "Pastoral Authority: A Study of the Authority of the Presbyterian Minister in Pastoral Care, Including Some Opinions of Ministers and Parishioners Regarding Aspects of Pastoral Behavior, and the Implications for a Doctrine of Church and Ministry and the Practice of Pastoral Care" (Th.D. diss., Princeton Theological Seminary, 1968).

46. *Ibid.*, p. 18.

47. *Ibid.*, p. 179. (The doctrinal considerations are explored in Ch. 3 of the dissertation, and the historical in Ch. 4. The first two points are self-evident, but the empirical study in Chs. 5 and 6 offers indirect support for them.)

48. "The majority of the words for 'obey' are the same, or connected with, words for 'hear' or 'listen.'" Carl Darling Buck, *A Dictionary of Selected Synonyms in the Principal Indo-European Languages: A Contribution to the History of Ideas* (The University of Chicago Press, 1949), p. 1339.

49. McIntosh, "Pastoral Authority," pp. 13 f. Other authors give the impression that the existence of authority in any given instance is dependent on compliance, and not merely on recognition. Cf. Gotthard Booth, "Problems of Authority for Individual Christians: Its Use and Abuse," *Journal of Pastoral Care*, Vol. VIII (1954), pp. 203–217; and Clyde H. Reid,

"Toward a Definition of Authority," *Journal of Religion and Health,* Jan., 1967, pp. 7–16.

50. Clinebell, *op. cit.,* p. 30.

51. McIntosh, "Pastoral Authority," pp. 165–167. The technical term is from Robert P. Abelson, "Modes of Resolution of Belief Dilemmas," in Martin Fishbein, *Readings in Attitude Theory and Measurement* (John Wiley & Sons, Inc., 1967), pp. 349–356.

52. Historically, the Reformed congregation originally had some responsibility for oversight of the pastor. According to *The First Book of Discipline:* "Yf a Minister be licht in conversation, by his Elderis and Seniouris, he aught to be admonished. Yf he be negligent in studie, or one that vaketh not upon his charge and flocke, or one that proponeth not frutefull doctrine, he deserveth scharper admonitioun and correctioun." James L. Ainslie, *The Doctrine of Ministerial Order in the Sixteenth and Seventeenth Centuries* (Edinburgh: T. & T. Clark, 1940), pp. 47 f. However, the Scottish Church soon ruled that only presbytery and higher courts should have authority over the minister, and this practice of oversight by the congregation did not continue (formally!).

53. McIntosh, "Pastoral Authority," pp. 150 ff.

54. Hiltner, *op. cit.,* pp. 20–29.

55. In other words, the context in which it is sought to establish the validity of pastoral theology renders it unnecessary to pursue the logically prior question of the nature of theological language. With respect to the assertions of a belief system, the criteria for validation required by the believer and the nonbeliever are not identical. Here it is the *intragroup* validity that has to be established, among those who accept the basic validity of theological language. This point and many of the others in this section were first made in McIntosh, "Pastoral Authority," pp. 40–68.

56. Daniel Day Williams, "Truth in the Theological Perspective," *Journal of Religion,* Vol. XXVIII, Oct., 1948, p. 250.

57. With regard to the help that the Reformers gave toward

the solution of the problem of authority, Davies observes: "The value of that assistance is diminished at the outset by one important fact: whereas everyone who reflects nowadays on the problem must regard as a possible answer the suggestion that there is no one in the age with which we are concerned who either conceived such a solution or would have considered it for a single moment. All thinkers, whether they were Catholics, Lutherans, Anabaptists, Zwinglians, Calvinists, Socinians, or whatever they were, agreed with one voice that there is an authoritative source of religious truth; the question that divided them was: what is it?" Rupert E. Davies, *The Problem of Authority in the Continental Reformers: A Study in Luther, Zwingli, and Calvin* (London: Epworth Press, 1946), p. 12.

58. The phrase is from Ian G. Barbour, *Issues in Science and Religion* (Prentice-Hall, Inc., 1966), p. 235.

59. Williams, *loc. cit.*, p. 149.

60. The illustration is assumed to be a matter of general knowledge, familiar to most Americans. The author became acquainted with it through watching the film *The Court-martial of Billy Mitchell.*

61. "The method of correlation explains the contents of the Christian faith through existential questions and theological answers in mutual interdependence." Tillich, *op. cit.*, Vol. I, p. 67. It is a fairly common observation that Tillich does not adhere rigorously to his stated method. Cf. Robert C. Kimball, "Implications of the Thought of Tillich and Freud for Relating Theology and Psychotherapy" (Ph.D. diss., Harvard University, 1959), pp. 201–206.

62. Oden, *op. cit.*

63. This is in no sense to dispute the finality of the work of Christ. It is to be understood in accordance with the statement: "According to the New Testament, the mission of Christ does not require to be taken over, for it is complete; what he accomplishes is sufficient once for all. It requires only to be communicated to men." George S. Hendry, *The Holy Spirit in Christian Theology,* rev. and enlarged ed. (The Westminster

Press, 1965), p. 64. But though the work of the Holy Spirit is of an essentially reproductive nature, it is nonetheless vital. "The Spirit is the subjective complement or counterpart of the objective fact of Christ, and it is the function of the Spirit to bring about an inner experience of the outward fact in the hearts of men." *Ibid.*, p. 25.

64. I am not aware of any systematic consideration of the problem in this form. Perhaps one of the criteria for such a distinction would be the inherent difficulty of objective judgment "in process," which was presumably the reason that "Modern History" as taught at Oxford University in the 1950's ended at 1914.

65. Jaroslav Pelikan, *Development of Christian Doctrine: Some Historical Prolegomena* (Yale University Press, 1969), p. 1.

66. *Ibid.*, p. 31.

67. *Ibid.*, pp. 144, 143.

68. It would appear that both Cyprian in his development of the doctrine of original sin (in the context of pastoral counsel on the practical question of when infants should be baptized), and Athanasius in his extrapolation from the ideal of the Christian virgin to the doctrine about Mary the Virgin (on the empirical basis of the earliest nuns of fourth-century Egypt), are implicitly claiming far *more* for the life and work of the church as a valid basis for constructive theology than is being asked in the present essay. Cf. Pelikan, *op. cit.*, pp. 82–91 and 100–104.

69. Cf. *Pastoral Psychology*, June, 1958, where Rogers takes issue with Niebuhr.

70. The case already referred to under "Pastoral Theology" in Chapter I, above, served this function. It led me to become aware of the paucity of the attention given to *seeking* forgiveness, despite the thousands upon thousands of words in the Bible and Christian literature on the subject of forgiveness. So stark is the contrast that it would not be too absurd to draw the inference that Christians think they are hardly ever in the wrong!

71. Reinhold Niebuhr, *The Nature and Destiny of Man: A Christian Interpretation* (London: James Nisbet & Co., Ltd., 1941). (The first surprise on turning to this two-volume work was to discover that only thirty pages are devoted to the whole analysis of pride!)

72. Reinhold Niebuhr, *op. cit.*, Vol. I, p. 200.

73. *Ibid.*, p. 190.

74. *Ibid.*, p. 193.

75. *Ibid.*, pp. 194 f.

76. *Ibid.*, p. 200. "The third type, the pride of self-righteousness, rises to a form of spiritual pride, which is at once a fourth type and yet not a specific form of pride at all but pride and self-glorification in its inclusive and quintessential form." *Ibid.*

77. *Ibid.*, p. 201.

78. *Ibid.*

79. *Ibid.*

80. *Ibid.*, p. 205.

81. *Ibid.*, p. 216.

82. Tertullian, *De Speculatis*, Ch. 1, cited by Reinhold Niebuhr, *op. cit.*, Vol. I, p. 218.

83. Reinhold Niebuhr, *op. cit.*, Vol. I, p. 219.

84. *Ibid.*, p. 218.

85. *Ibid.*, p. 194.

86. *Ibid.*, pp. 208 ff. His point here is clearly different from ours, however. "Group pride, though having its source in individual attitudes, actually achieves a certain authority over the individual and results in unconditioned demands by the group upon the individual." *Ibid.*, p. 208.

87. Emil Brunner, *Man in Revolt* (The Westminster Press, 1947), p. 132.

88. Peter Homans, *Theology After Freud: An Interpretive Inquiry* (Bobbs-Merrill Company, Inc., 1970), p. 61.

89. *Ibid.*

90. Bernard M. Loomer, "Empirical Theology Within Process Thought," in Bernard E. Meland (ed.), *The Future of Empiri-*

*cal Theology* (The University of Chicago Press, 1969), p. 169.

91. *Ibid.*, p. 156.

92. The Greek word *elpis* was originally quite equivocal and used rather generally for expectations of the future, needing qualification as *elpis agathe* to mean "hope" in our modern sense. In the Septuagint and New Testament, however, there is no neutral concept of *elpis*. "On the contrary to hope and to fear (with the future in view) are differentiated in the language from the first." Rudolf Bultmann and Karl Heinrich Rengstorf, *Bible Key Words: From Gerhard Kittel's Theologisches Wörterbuch zum Neuen Testament*, Vol. V: *Hope* (London: A. & C. Black, Ltd., 1963), p. 9.

93. Jürgen Moltmann, *The Theology of Hope: On the Ground and the Implications of a Christian Eschatology* (Harper & Row, Publishers, Inc., 1967), p. 16.

94. *Ibid.*, p. 33.

95. In assessing the merits and continuing problems of the new "theology of hope," Migliore has stated: "2. A more pointed criticism of the theology of hope is that its anthropological assumptions remain undeveloped. . . . While deeply indebted to Bloch's study, Moltmann's *Theology of Hope* makes surprisingly little explicit use of the analyses of man's capacities of dreaming, imagining, anticipating, etc., which fill the pages of Bloch's writing and which provide some definition of the understanding of man presupposed by Moltmann and other theologians of hope. . . ." Daniel L. Migliore, "The 'Theology of Hope' in Perspective," *Princeton Seminary Bulletin*, Summer, 1968, p. 49.

96. While including additional material, an earlier attempt by the present writer to piece together an appraisal of human hoping will be drawn on freely. Cf. Ian F. McIntosh, "The Riddle of Pandora's Box," *Austin Seminary Bulletin*, April, 1969, pp. 5–16.

97. Gaylin has made a strong case for the essence of despair being a loss of self-confidence, the loss of confidence in the operating capacity of the ego and its ability to cope. This is

clearly not true of Mrs. Jackson. Cf. Willard Gaylin, *op. cit.*, pp. 388 f. The striking question is *why* has Mrs. Jackson not yet succumbed to a sense of helplessness. This is beyond the scope of the present inquiry, but two possibilities may be noted. One is that Mrs. Jackson attributed the cause of all the misfortunes to persons or things outside herself. The other is that her experiences may have led her to expect success to follow even numerous failures. Cf. Ezra Stotland, *The Psychology of Hope: An Integration of Experimental, Clinical, and Social Approaches* (Jossey-Bass Inc., Publishers, 1969), pp. 55, 70.

98. Moltmann, *op. cit.*, p. 23.

99. *Ibid.*

100. Stotland, *op. cit.*, p. 2, has as a definition: "The essence of . . . hope is an expectation greater than zero of achieving a goal." Moltmann seems to be saying that the expectation of achieving something one longs for *cannot* be zero, but if it is less than 10 percent, say, one may pretend that it is. This is similar to an explanation that the author has heard somewhere for the dynamics of skepticism.

101. Moltmann, *op. cit.*, p. 17. It must be doubted, however, whether Moltmann's attempt to distinguish eschatology from all other doctrines (in that "hope's statements of promise . . . do not result from experiences") can be upheld. For not only must the ground of hope have been experienced, but, as will be seen, the content is generally (though not specifically) defined by the ground. *Ibid.*, p. 18.

102. *Ibid.*, p. 20.

103. Gabriel Marcel, *Homo Viator: Introduction to a Metaphysic of Hope,* tr. by Emma Craufurd (Henry Regnery Co., 1951), p. 32.

104. Paul W. Pruyser, "Phenomenology and Dynamics of Hoping," *Journal for the Scientific Study of Religion,* Oct., 1963, p. 87.

105. Stotland, *op. cit.*, p. 19. However, it is not clear that Stotland has left no room for the Christian hope by the support

he marshals for this hypothesis. "We see then that data from controlled laboratory experiments, on both humans and on animals, from schools, from peacetime disaster, from hospitals, from concentration and prisoner-of-war camps, all point to the importance of hope for action." *Ibid.*, p. 22. What he does not demonstrate is the importance of action for hope—especially when that hope is dependent upon factors or persons that cannot be influenced.

106. Moltmann, *op. cit.*, p. 23.

107. Pruyser, *loc. cit.*, p. 89.

108. Moltmann, *op. cit.*, p. 25.

109. Pruyser, *loc. cit.*, pp. 92 f.

110. *Ibid.*, p. 94.

111. McIntosh, "The Riddle of Pandora's Box," p. 6.

112. Moltmann, *op. cit.*, pp. 26 f.

113. McIntosh, "The Riddle of Pandora's Box," p. 8.

114. Friedrich Schleiermacher, *The Christian Faith*, Eng. tr. of the 2d German ed., ed. by H. R. Mackintosh and J. S. Stewart (Edinburgh: T. & T. Clark, 1928), pp. 13 f.

115. *Ibid.*, p. 15.

116. Reinhold Niebuhr, *op. cit.*, Vol. I., p. 194.

117. *Ibid.*, p. 255.

118. *Ibid.*, p. 242.

119. Goldstein, *loc. cit.*, p. 38.

120. Tillich, *op. cit.*, Vol. III, p. 45.

121. Tillich, *op. cit.*, Vol. I, p. 195.

122. Tillich, *op. cit.*, Vol. III, pp. 76 f.

123. Tillich, *op. cit.*, Vol. II, p. 75.

124. Tillich, *op. cit.*, Vol. III, p. 33.

125. Richard R. Niebuhr, *Schleiermacher on Christ and Religion: A New Introduction* (Charles Scribner's Sons, 1964), p. 186.

126. *Ibid.*, p. 188.

127. Schleiermacher, *op. cit.*, p. 21.

128. *Ibid.*, p. 24.